# THE
# MOTLEY
# FOOL
# WHAT TO DO
# WITH YOUR
# MONEY
# NOW

## Ten Steps to
## Staying Up in
## a Down Market

# David and
# Tom Gardner

A FIRESIDE BOOK
PUBLISHED BY SIMON & SCHUSTER
NEW YORK LONDON TORONTO SYDNEY SINGAPORE

FIRESIDE
Rockefeller Center
1230 Avenue of the Americas
New York, NY 10020

First Fireside edition 2003
FIRESIDE and colophon are registered trademarks
of Simon & Schuster, Inc.

The Motley Fool and the Jester logo are registered trademarks
of The Motley Fool, Inc.

For information about special discounts for bulk purchases,
please contact Simon & Schuster Special Sales:
1-800-456-6798 or business@simonandschuster.com.

Designed by Karolina Harris

Manufactured in the United States of America

10  9  8  7  6  5  4  3  2  1

The Library of Congress has cataloged the Simon & Schuster edition as follows:
Gardner, David, date.
The Motley Fool's what to do with your money now : ten steps to staying up in
a down market / David and Tom Gardner.
    p. cm.
  Includes index.
  1. Investments.  2. Finance, Personal.  I. Title: What to do with your money now.
II. Gardner, Tom, date.  III. Motley Fool, Inc.  IV. Title.

HG4521. G193 2002
332.6—dc21                                              2002021722

ISBN 0-7432-3378-6
    0-7432-3465-0 (Pbk)

*This book honors the contributions of those many people we laid off from our business in the year 2001, among them beloved friends and family members, a human congeries of passion and talent.*

# ACKNOWLEDGMENTS

While every word herein writ is ours (with the exception of the community postings which so enrich the text), books don't just happen thanks to an author or two. Listing only the authors' names on the cover is the equivalent of listing only the lead actors' names in movie credits. Thus:

Thanks and glory be to the ever-growing family of Fools—our several-million-strong Fool.com online visitors, our membership, our radio listeners, newspaper and book readers. And our actual family, and friends, and family of friendly employees. You inspire us, and we thank you for your stories and for your suggestions about how to improve execution of our chosen mission: to educate, to amuse, and to enrich.

We tip our belled caps to our agent, Suzanne Gluck, for her enthusiasm and continued persistence in helping two Fools stumble through the publishing world.

We extend our appreciation to Geoff Kloske, our editor at Simon & Schuster, for his guidance and patience in bringing this book from concept to print. And, Geoff, do you ever get angry with people? Stop being so easy-going.

Also, the copyediting team of Isolde Sauer and Fred Chase from Simon & Schuster for crossing the t's and dotting the i's, but leaving our darned o's alone. Isolde, this is book number six together—ready for six more? Who's going to outlast whom?

And back in the open and nurturing environment of Fool HQ, we'd again like to thank all our staff for persevering during a bumpy 2001 and putting up with their two guys who had occasional deadlines to meet and couldn't always find time to clean up the kitchen and keep the candy jar filled. (Thanks, Alex.) For research help and project management on this book, we'd especially like to thank Rex Moore, Jonathan Mudd, Brian Bauer, Melissa Flaim, Reggie Santiago, Mona Sharma, and Alissa Territo.

# CONTENTS

# PREFACE

This book is a grab bag.

It began initially as a direct response to a bear market and a troubled world. In the midst of unprecedented national instability, many of us have watched our portfolios drop and our years until retirement rise. And thus we wrote the middle section, first, "What to Do Now."

But then we realized that a book that merely addressed present circumstance—particularly ever-changing present circumstance—lacked some warranted reflection about the past. "How did we all get into this mess in the first place? What factors led to such a significant economic and financial decline?" These were questions we wanted to take a crack at answering, and so next we wrote the first section, "What Happened?"

With the past and present covered, it seemed only right to close this short tome pointing ahead to the future. We all have resolutions coming out of such a bad two years in the life of our country; we wanted to share ours. And hence, "What Next?"

For some, perhaps only one of the sections is useful. For others, two or even all three sections may have utility, or merit, or both. Regardless, we hope you find at least one tip in this little book that more than covers *its* cost, and, more important, the *hidden and deeper cost* of the time you put into reading it.

With Foolish best wishes for a prosperous 2002 and beyond.

# THE
# MOTLEY FOOL
# WHAT TO DO
# WITH YOUR
# MONEY
# NOW

# INTRODUCTION

Should auld acquaintance be forgot,
And never brought to mind?
— ROBERT BURNS, "Auld Lang Syne"

Widely published business theorist Peter Drucker criticized the career of Apple cofounder Steve Jobs by stating that Jobs met with too much success in the first five years of his career. Consequently, he never really had to make "the tough decisions." And when later he and his company did get in a bind, during the encroachment of new manager John Sculley, it became too easy, acceptable, and perhaps convenient for Jobs to part, quit, walk away. Start NeXT Software. Start Pixar. Come back to Apple on a white horse.

Drucker's rap on Jobs is that he hasn't truly experienced what it's like to stick it out through the difficult times and rebuild.[1]

---

[1] Well, one of us is on record for having written the occasional paean to Steve Jobs as a great American entrepreneur. So we can't both countenance these criticisms of Jobs, and one of us (David) notes with pleasure the creative and commercial success of movies like *Toy Story* and *Monsters, Inc*. We hereby formally suggest that Pixar be dubbed "the animation studio that never made a flop."

We have three observations about Drucker's comment. Consider that in our own much smaller way we have now mirrored portions of Jobs's early career, having as young men started a succès fou (pun intended), featuring best-selling books, magazine covers, a national radio show now on NPR, a syndicated newspaper column in virtually every noteworthy paper in this country, having raised $2 million through revolutionary online giving campaigns we call Foolanthropy, and (also to be noted, with appropriate catcalls as well) having raised tens of millions of dollars of venture capital to help The Motley Fool grow into an international name. Market research done in the year 2000 suggested that fully one third of all people ever to have used the World Wide Web had visited our Motley Fool online service, which is open to more business than ever today at Fool.com (please join in the fun, if you haven't already).

All that, self-made, in our twenties and now early thirties.

Whoa! Hold on! Is that our first observation? You paid your 23 bucks just to read some random brag?

Hardly—the above was just context. Our first observation is that Drucker can't level his Jobsian criticism at us because we have stuck around, straight through what has been a business and investing nightmare full of nosediving advertising rates, a nosediving stock market, numerous employee goodbyes, and almost unrelenting stress for the past two years.

And it's not fun. We think—nay, we know—that Jobs is smarter than we are.

Which is the second observation.

The third and most important observation concerns you. It is that the business and investing climate have probably treated you very similarly—perhaps (we hope) a little bit better, perhaps a little bit worse. The point is, we have all been through something like a nightmare together. As we Fools tipped our glasses at a family retreat in Vermont during the darkening eve of December 31, 2001, it was the first time in memory that we looked into the eyes of family and friends all around us and found that they shared back the same unusual, unanimous twinkle: GOOD RIDDANCE, 2001!!! (And 2000, for that matter.)

Our epigraph above from "Auld Lang Syne" was thus chosen for its irony. Indeed, we said goodbye via layoffs to so many old acquaintances in the year 2001. Our answer to the poet is that if we're not allowed to forget auld acquaintance, we would like to forget virtually everything else about the past two years.

Except that we can't. Because none of us can afford to.


This is a book for you, the person in our society hoping to learn from the mistakes of the past, hoping most of all to make a better decision about your money. We've entitled it *What to Do with Your Money Now* because that's exactly what we're here to shed light on, to provide you the necessary steps you can and should take now, toward the latter stages of a nasty bear market. We lead off appropriately with "What Happened?" before moving into "What to Do Now" and closing with "What Next?" We've kept this short and sweet, alternately step-oriented and digressive. It's a motley book.

But it's also a book coming to you from two fellow investors turned entrepreneurs, who feel along with Warren Buffett that we're better investors because we're businessmen, and better businessmen because we're investors. And so in what we hope is a completely accessible and anecdotal manner, this book is also a bit of a business book, containing as it does some stories of our own business and what we've personally learned, and become better at, as a result of an unthinkably horrible beginning to the new millennium.

Now you may be wondering, why would I take advice from guys in Fool caps? We've heard that from day one when we titled our original newsletter in July of 1993 *The Motley Fool*. And we shall probably hear it, regardless, till kingdom come. We'll continue to say simply that we choose to wear our caps because our Foolish goal remains the same as those of the cap-wearing court jesters of yore: to tell our audience the truth about a difficult subject, doing so in terms that are refreshingly blunt, often contrary, and always (we hope) pleasing, mixing in a spoonful of amusement to help the medicine go down. You may further be wondering why you should take advice from guys in Fool caps who watched their own portfolios get cut in half over the past two years. Our reply is that virtually anyone who invests patiently in growth companies had the same thing happen through this period in which the Nasdaq lost an unprecedented 60 percent plus of its value. (The good news for long-term investors is that the decade leading up to 2000–2001 was so wonderful that even 50 percent down leaves a trace of a smile on our faces.) You may finally wonder what business savvy could possibly come from two guys in Fool caps who watched their stock portfolio get cut in half over the past two years and had to significantly shrink their employee base in the past year.

Well, two reasons, we suppose.

The first comes via a cheery longtime businessman and neighbor of ours, who remarked one spring 2001 morning as we drove in to work that "anyone who survives the next six months will make it through the next twenty years." In other words, guiding one's company through the past few seasons and having anything left at all is a blessing (and you were right, Jim; and if you, dear reader, are in business you know what we mean—Enron employees in particular). And second, you may also be comforted to know that your authors consciously and continually rejected any temptation and numerous outside urges to take our company, The Motley Fool, public.

That should say a lot, because it meant a lot. We didn't go public. Thank God. We didn't rush to cash in on—or out of—our business through a period during which that became all the rage, exposing the quick-buck motivations of many who left the messy mop-up and accompanying losses to the next investor, the greater "fool" (small "f"!)—as the parlance would have it. Instead, we kept control of the thing we loved: our company and its mission.

Let's get on with the book.

# PART ONE

# WHAT
# HAPPENED?

The most advantageous first step into the future is one whose direction is informed by a knowledge of the past. The recent past is the stuff of history books, a period that saw the growth, massive proliferation, and fast decline of hundreds of companies that raised and blew billions of dollars. Jeffrey Bezos of Amazon.com accurately likened this period to the Cambrian explosion in biology, when a higher level of oxygen and other environmental factors gave rise to a huge increase in the creation of new species—and then not long after (in biological terms) a huge number of extinctions.

That is what has happened on a smaller scale, in a financial way, millions of years later. We as a society of investors and businesspeople are still sifting through the wreckage. We owe it to ourselves to look hard at what lessons we might draw both from how things happened and why they happened, in order that we might do better in the future.

In five chapters, then, this section explores five reasons why our economy and stock market hit severe downturns. We are not journalists, or bean counters. We aren't going to list the number of businesses that failed, because it's enough for us to note that too many did . . . and that many should never have been loosed upon the public markets in the first place. No, we're not here to document events that all of us already know anyway, having just lived through them. Instead, we're here as two authors—who were themselves winning and losing in the middle of the arena—to examine the bust that followed the boom of the 1990s. And as is probably the ultimate reason underlying any bust, we believe this one ultimately reflects a failure of character. We think behind the financings, the products and services, the ubiquitous (and often quite good) television advertising from businesses that didn't have meaningful revenues yet—behind all these things, are people—people who, many of them, were actually well intentioned. But people who were flawed for one or more of several reasons. If you dig deeply enough, you'll perhaps agree with us that it is ultimately these character flaws that lead markets and economies to new lows. And it is these lessons we do well to learn as, well, people.

That's why each chapter in our opening section details one particular, relevant character failure broadly shared by investors and businesspeople.

Each of the five chapters' analyses works on both a business and investing level. In other words, the first point, "We were impatient," portrays a business world that was manufacturing IPOs right alongside an investor world hell-bent on striking it rich overnight. Business and investing are so often just two faces of the same coin (call that coin "making money," if you like), hence our inclusion of complementary lessons in each chapter. We've chosen to lead off with the business lesson each time because as we'll say later we're business-focused investors. We believe that if you get your business thinking right (an opportunity open to anyone with a brain), your investment success will follow.

Examples in this first section are drawn from mistakes that well-known public companies made, and mistakes that we as investors and managers of a high-profile Internet business made. By the end of this introductory section, we hope to have helped you toward understanding why things played out as they did—why American business practices could possibly have led to 1.3 million layoffs over the past two years, as Reuters has reported—arming you with info and the right perspective for not repeating these mistakes.

# 1
# We
# Were
# Impatient

A *New York Times* cartoon from the late 1990s perfectly captured the spirit of the age. Entitled "How to Start Your Very Own Silicon Valley Startup," its captions went thus:

STEP ONE:   Go to Menlo Park. Find a tree.

STEP TWO:   Shake the tree. A venture capitalist will drop out. Before he regains his wits, recite the following incantation: "Internet, Electronic Commerce, Distributed Enterprise-Enabled Applications, Java!"

STEP THREE: The venture capitalist will give you $4 million.

STEP FOUR:  In 18 months, go public.

STEP FIVE:  After you receive your check, go back to Menlo Park. Find a tree.

STEP SIX:   Climb it. Wait.

That is the environment that all of us were living through, and in which many of us were investing and working.

We were impatient.

The macro business environment was impatient.

And this point, like each of the points in this section, provides us both a business and investing lesson.

## THE BUSINESS LESSON

As co-chairmen of the Motley Fool, we can say that we felt a tremendous amount of pressure—both externally and internally—to grow grow grow. We suspect we're not the only ones. For our business, that meant selling a portion of it to venture capitalists to fund new growth. As a small private company founded in 1993, we had a brief history of profitability generated solely by our own resources. And yet we came to realize that we had an international opportunity, and so decided to raise more than $20 million in financing. Our plan was to spend that money to grow toward a second round of financing, in which we would raise even more money. And we did. And we tip our belled caps to our investors, Maveron, AOL Time Warner, Mayfield, and Softbank, for providing us the opportunity to grow and reach many more Fools. And then spend that again to grow further, at which point would come a hypothetical third round that would be even more than that. Having raised that final round, we would turn profitable, retaining about half of that money, and then take our company to the public markets.

It was the way we thought of things. It was the Zeitgeist, the modus operandi, the short but well-worn path.

But step away and ask yourself, "How does good business happen? And how is something created that will be both profitable and sustainable over a long period of time?" What was just described above—with its forced-march progress, its emphasis on raising money rather than building a business model, its expectation of inevitable refinancing (what was passing for the modus operandi) was in fact a very unusual standard.

How did this happen? How did the world come to think this way? We need look no further than the development and growth of the Internet. The rapid and unprecedented revolution in technology that would lead to a global network, and all the new possibilities it promised, easily explains why lots of money was invested in companies like ours. Many companies across all of American business enjoyed major boosts in valuation. And yet there was an overweening impatience to it all . . . stocks and valuations rose to breathtaking levels, creating a collectively felt need to justify the multiples by turbocharging your growth—or your growth expectations, if you were an investor.

For our own business, this rapid growth and influx of financing meant we needed a CEO, our first-ever, who wound up being Pat Garner. Pat had spent his previous thirty-five years as a manager and marketer at Coca-Cola. He brought along an intense numerical focus into our company. "Guys— if you can't measure it, you can't manage it."

Up until then, until the past twelve months, we just didn't think we had time to be numerical. We had to raise more money, take the Motley Fool mission of financial responsibility to more countries, and continue to grow grow grow.

And then we got a visit to Fool HQ from author and consultant Steven Cristol (author of the useful business book *Simplicity Marketing,* Free Press, 2000). Steven told us, "I was impatient for success in another career. I was, at the time, a Silicon Valley marketing consultant. And yet my dream was to be a songwriter.

"So here's what I did. I went to Los Angeles, which is where anyone who dreams of being a songwriter goes. And everyone thought I was crazy. My family thought I was crazy, but they followed me. For two to three years I just mixed around and tried to meet the right people and wrote songs. Nothing worked. I became increasingly impatient for success. And then, as luck would have it, I finally got a lunch date with a Big Honcho. So beforehand, I checked in with a friend of mine who knew the industry and I said, 'Here's my opportunity. I'm allowed to put together a demo tape of three songs, give it to the Big Honcho, and maybe finally create my big break. So I'm thinking of throwing him three different looks. A fast song, a slow song, something in between. And—' "

And his friend cut him off. "Steven, that's what everyone does. When we're impatient for success we tend to do what everyone else does. Here's my suggestion to you: one song. Pick your best song. Whatever is your best song put just that on the tape and send it to the guy. Because anything else you do will dilute that. And by the very act of just sending one song you will stand out to that particular gentleman more than all the other dozens of songwriters he's talking to this month."

And for Steven Cristol, as he went on to tell us, that approach led to his first gold album. And he went on and had success as a songwriter with a few gold records . . . and eventually returned to Silicon Valley as a marketing consultant. (What does that say about the songwriting industry?) Impatient for success, Steven Cristol nevertheless avoided his initial tendency to do what everyone else was doing and instead met with great success.

Impatient groupthink has hurt a lot of businesses in the past few years. So, as we look back and ask, "What happened?" we hope we're learning patience—patience, say, in the form of spending money that you already have as opposed to spending money you expect to have.

One universally renowned venture capitalist firm we met with was so deeply infected by this groupthink that when we sat down with them to share our story in early 1999, their sole question, asked up front, was, "How did you guys blow it?" We wondered how they thought we'd blown it. "Why didn't you go public first? Why did you let a bunch of competitors get out there [i.e., to the public markets] before you did?"

In their minds, that was the mark of success. An early initial public offering (IPO). A "preemptive IPO," perhaps. Never mind that the firms they were referring to are now, just three years later, either wilting or out of business altogether. It wouldn't matter to the venture capitalists much, anyway. They're usually the sellers on IPO day; those were their shares the public was buying.

Which, we suppose, is the point. The business side of that point.

## THE INVESTING LESSON

We were also very impatient as investors. Many invested in businesses whose products and services they weren't immediately familiar with, perhaps out of fear of missing the rocket ride. As we now know, companies like Pets.com, Cyberian Outpost, and theglobe.com rode only briefly, before vanishing. More than 300 companies that could be classified primarily as Internet businesses went public in the 1990s. Over 80 percent of them had less than five years of operating history. That's public market money they took (perhaps yours), under the implied oath to grow their businesses indefinitely, limitlessly—the promise that any public company makes to its shareholders.

If you've really only been around for fifteen months, that's a very difficult promise to make.

But is it all their fault? Did these companies force investors to buy their shares? Was this in fact a criminal act perpetrated on a naive and blameless public? Perhaps you can see where we're going with this.

When people are in a hurry to invest, rarely will they distinguish between first- and third-tier technology companies. We know this because of the sheer number of investors that floated the valuations of companies like Drkoop.com to hundreds of millions—in some cases, billions—of dollars. Much of this buying was indiscriminate. Here's an example.

Take the spin-off of Palm on March 2, 2000. Longtime networking gear company 3Com had a hot property, full ownership of Palm Inc., the company behind the fast-growing line of Palm personal digital assistants. That day, 3Com sold 5 percent of its stake in Palm Inc. to the public markets, an IPO that was offered at $38 per share and closed the day at $95 (reaching as high as $145!). The day's close valued Palm at an implied market capitalization of $53.5 billion. We at Fool HQ were not the only ones to wonder aloud on our online site how Palm could be worth $53.5 billion, when the day before, 3Com in its entirety had only been worth about half that.

Let it not be said that so-called full-service brokerage firms don't still have great influence over the buying appetites and habits of their customers. Many a phone was pounded many a time that day.

You wanna buy 5 percent of this book? Or 5 percent of our wardrobe? 5 percent of our company? 5 percent of anything of ours that we can sell you? This paragraph brought to you by what we've learned from 3Com. Anyway, if you ever did want to buy 5 percent of something, we assume you'd want to know what that thing was worth. If so, you'd have done more homework than, in all likelihood, the purchasers of Palm stock did that first day. It was enough, it seems, to "get in on the Palm IPO." (Whatever the price.) Just to have some "hot shares" of a "hot IPO." (Whatever the price.) We love strong brand names and the companies behind them as much as the next guy . . . but not at whatever the price.

With so many indiscriminate buyers simply wanting in, perhaps it's not surprising that just a month later the Nasdaq Composite began what would represent a greater than 60 percent decline over the succeeding eighteen months—unprecedented, the Nasdaq never having dropped so far. As the market closed the Friday of this writing, Palm traded 16 million shares and closed at $3.47—pricing the entity at about $2 billion—about one one-twenty-fourth of its IPO day closing value, less than two years ago. 3Com, itself in tatters, is priced roughly the same. By the way, 3Com dished out its remaining ownership of Palm in July of 2000. Investors still paid a sizable premium then compared to what the company is worth now. Of course, one can say that about many companies these days, after a bear market.

Now, who do you think was doing this indiscriminate buying? The answer is that most of us were. While we two brothers didn't ever own any Palm, David paid a pretty penny once for @Home (later "Excite@Home," David recalls with a shudder) and Tom held his Yahoo! up to $237 and back down again (much further down than up). Perhaps you have a few of your own. We suspect that if you're a baby boomer, you might have several.

There can be no question that a lot of the market's juice and then its later sputter comes to us courtesy of the baby boom generation. With so many coming to grips with their own mortality and also with their own lack of retirement preparation, for baby boomers the stock market became the logical "go-to" solution to the conundrum, "How can I retire comfortably and soon if I'm forty-six, am still in debt, and haven't thought about investing until, um, now?" The stock market, with its superior historical returns and close tie to technology and its resultant prosperity, was a great answer. America's promise, her emerging dominance in global technology, and spirit of free market capitalism made it only more attractive. (We've written a book or two about that, and feel just as strongly now as we did back then about the net benefits of the system.) But the impatience of a large generation of people who are in their peak earning years and control most of the country's assets probably cannot be overemphasized when we consider what happened. The 20 percent plus annual performance of the stock market through 1995–97 can only have further steeled the will and confidence of this generation to invest invest invest right alongside all of us who were trying to grow grow grow.

Again, much of this represents good intentions and sometimes good results—taken in moderation. The problem was that the stock market's bright supernova continued to light up the skies in 1998–99, giving us all too much, too soon. And the deeper truth is, had America traditionally and effectively educated its citizens about finance and money, our country wouldn't have so many debtors, so many people who lack any notion of the stock market's historic performance until it begins to look so good they figure they'll now finally take a shot on that pony too.

Attempting to prey upon this very mentality in order to teach a lesson about it, we decided to do something different at Fool.com on April Fool's Day. The day was April 1, 1999 (for reasons evident, our national holiday). We closed down all the options available to people coming to our Web site and instead announced on our main page that The Motley Fool was going in a compelling new direction. With many so-called Internet companies worth a couple billion dollars after just a year of being in business, we had decided to give our community a chance to invest in one. No, not ours. But one that we believed in, believed in so much that The Motley Fool was entering the underwriting business for the benefit of its customers, so that they could get in early on a hot IPO for once, instead of all those darned institutions.

And so on April 1, 1999, eMeringue.com was born.

At the risk of already beginning to sound in some way plausible, we'll run the lesser risk of repeating ourselves: This was all an April Fool's joke—this is not an actual company. We were attempting to teach a lesson throughout the day about the overenthusiasm surrounding unknown businesses that had dot-com as their suffix.

So at 9:45 A.M. we announced eMeringue was live on the Halifax Canadian Exchange, ticker symbol HAFD. We urged our readers to consider going out and buying shares right away, before the rest of the world discovered the eMeringue magic. "If you've been a veteran user of our site," we wrote, "you know that we think you should do your own research and make your own decisions. But on this one day, in this one hour, we at The Motley Fool have done your research for you. We believe in eMeringue so much that we've underwritten it, and at market open we have issued a Strong Buy recommendation on shares of eMeringue."

eMeringue's business was of course not the pie, not the filling, just the meringue on top, delivered from a click on its Web site to anywhere in the continental U.S., in seven days or less. (Can you imagine, by the way, the tasty experience of seven-day-old crystallized meringue whip?) And yes, we created a whole Web site for it, brought to life by an in-house creative team led by our incredibly talented associate Todd Etter. In fact, it's still up there, recipes and all—please visit eMeringue.com, experience the Eggulator, try out an order form, and take a tour of the e-process led by friendly cartoon character Marty Meringue.

Of course, we're thinking as we develop this in the days before that no one is going to fall for our April Fool's joke. But with merry aplomb we proceed with the script, anyway, including tricking up our site so that you can get live "real" quotations of eMeringue all day long.

The live graph of the stock price at Fool.com told quite a tale that day. That morning the stock, offered at $22 a share, opened at $84. An outstanding IPO! (One of so many, that year.) Congratulations to the shareholders of eMeringue and particularly to our friends, the executive team (including CEO Larry McCloskey), with whom we worked so hard to realize this dream. At 11:00 A.M., the stock crests $149 and executives gather and announce, effective the following Monday, a three-for-one stock split.

(Sarcasm Alert—it being the wit of Fools: This event naturally gave us an opportunity to tell people our most important piece of investment advice, which is always buy on a stock split. Stock splits create a lot of value in a business, you know. You definitely wanted to get in right then and buy more shares of eMeringue.com before Monday.)

(If you didn't detect sarcasm in the previous paragraph because you do believe stock splits create value, we encourage you to report directly to our Fool's School at Fool.com, or read pages 238–40 of our *Motley Fool Money Guide* to get the straight stuff on the relative meaninglessness of stock splits.)

By noon, shares were up to $218, and eMeringue was launching a hostile takeover of another Web upstart, Cyber Crust. Said CEO McCloskey: "This will be the first step toward our five-year goal of producing an entire pie." But, unfortunately for him, that goal would never near realization.

With the shares at $319, at 1:30 P.M. the SEC announced that it had stumbled across "accounting irregularities" in the prospectus, and the shares began to nosedive. Even worse, 3:15 P.M. saw a report of a food poisoning scare in Wisconsin related to some meringues that eMeringue had shoveled out of its Boise, Idaho, home office. At 3:18 P.M., executives gathered again and announced effective immediately a one-for-ten reverse stock split to try and get the price back up. And at 4:00 P.M., eMeringue closed at . . . 84 cents a share.

What a day. A wild ride. And in retrospect, our creative team was presaging what would in fact happen in the financial world over the next two years. It's just that ours was a fiction, presented in accelerated form. It was all over by nightfall.

Again, we did not think that anyone would fall for our April Fool's joke. But throughout the day we got phone calls from big-name brokerage firms trying to find out what this company was. "Our clients are calling us. They want into this stock. Guys, can you help us out?" They couldn't find the ticker symbol; in fact, they couldn't even find the Halifax Canadian Exchange that the company was being traded on. One of their clients posted a note to our Fool.com discussion boards.* Written perhaps frantically, in all upper-case lettering, it read:

MY BROKER CAN'T FIND THE TICKER, CAN'T FIND THE COMPANY, CAN'T FIND THE EXCHANGE, WHAT SHOULD I DO?

And one of our veteran community contributors responded, to our surprise, "Your broker can't find the ticker, the company, or the exchange? What should you do? Fire your broker!" So we did have others helping us, playing along. (One wonders how the conversation fared between client and broker on April 2.)

We got more than 600 notes the next day. The best involved a wonderful running exchange between a husband and wife at different places of work throughout the day. They were arguing about whether they should buy shares. He was convinced that they should; they had missed, in his opinion, the technology run-up, partly because she had resisted taking risks in their portfolio. This was their chance. You can imagine his anger and frustration when HAFD shares (the ticker symbol stands for "Happy April Fool's Day" if you hadn't yet

*At Fool.com, we host many active conversations via our online community discussion boards. By posting messages to the boards, individual Fools can interact and learn together about a wide range of topics—financial, investing, and many other important facets of life. You can enjoy a 30-day free trial to the Fool Community to see what it's all about.

puzzled that one out) crossed $200 by noon. Anyway, as the shares began to fall she started taunting him. At 4:53 P.M., when CEO McCloskey was arrested trying to hijack a Carnival cruise line to Finland—he'd held three crew members hostage with a frosting gun—they both then realized it was a joke. They learned a lesson about taking their time as investors.

Which is the point of this chapter. Impatience leads to so many wrong things.

Perhaps some nameless *Seattle Times* staffer was guilty of impatience as well when, a few weeks later, the *Times* ran an article on the front page of their Living Section listing the top ten Web sites for food and cooking. With no trace of irony, they listed number three: eMeringue. The text read, "This has to be the best opening text ever written for a Web site: 'I'm Larry McCloskey, president and CEO of eMeringue. When I converted my Boise, Idaho, auto-parts dealership into a meringue-delivery service, I really had no idea we would grow to the size we are today. Forty-five employees. $11 million in revenue.' The guarantee here: delivery of a pie meringue to anywhere in the United States in seven days."

To close, whether we're talking about the fictional eMeringue, the very real Drkoop.com, the mistakes we made in our own business, or the ones you may have made in yours, the aim is to identify the root problems. One of those is certainly impatience. It's easy to get caught up in the emotions of the day and the seemingly great opportunity dangling right before our eyes. Probably only a small fraction of those who believed in eMeringue that fateful day really felt the company had any long-term prospects. Most just wanted to double their money in a single day. Eighty-four cents per share was the right lesson for them then, and is sadly similar to real experiences others of us have had since.

To recognize this now is to defeat it later.

# 2

# We
# Didn't Play
# Our Game

Celebrated fund manager and noted investment author Peter Lynch talks about this all the time: Buy what you know. Warren Buffett, the greatest investor of our time, says the same thing in a different way: Invest within your "circle of competence." In this chapter, we're going to call it "playing your game," alternatively, "maintaining your home-field advantage." No secret that professional sports teams win more games at home than they do away from home; it's a phenomenon repeated across all sports at all levels. We can debate why this is, what exactly is going on there. But there is no debate about whether it happens or not, whether it's real. It's very real, and this simple concept is sadly so often ignored or just plain missed by so many of us as we make decisions about our money.

What's good for the goose is good for the gander, and what's good advice for your investing is good advice for your business.

## THE BUSINESS LESSON

A lot of businesses started looking outside their circle of competence in order to expand. The example we know best is small and insignificant compared to most, but we know it the best because it was our own. Having launched our online service successfully with AOL in the early 1990s, we decided we had an almost magical ability to create engaging interactive services for large numbers of people across virtually any topic. Consequently, we took time out of building our financial site in 1995 to build out a sports site, a movie site, and a culture site on AOL (which, by the way, was a much smaller company back then). Based on the incredible amount of press and kudos coming in domestically and internationally about The Motley Fool, in our own minds the possibility even existed that we might come to dominate all content on AOL. (Er, this was before they bought Time Warner!)

So for the next two years we ended up spending a third to one half of our time and resources on these three new sites that, combined, had traffic just a fraction of that of our financial site, and with a much slower growth rate.

Were we playing our game?

Our former CEO Pat Garner provided us a helpful way of realizing "no":

"Guys, I want to tell you about the Big Arrow."

It's a graph. On one axis you plot "Opportunities," and on the other "Capabilities." The idea is to match your opportunities with your capabilities. The big arrow is the wide boulevard running northeast, which represents those initiatives that a company is well suited toward, those that match a

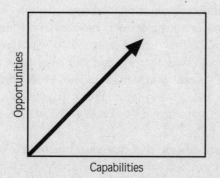

Capabilities

company's potential for growth with its ability to deliver. In the lower left you see smaller initiatives for which a company is suited, without being underqualified (unable to do them) or overqualified (wasting resources that could've been more effectively used elsewhere). Within the upper-right quadrant of the graph, you have the real meaning and purpose of the company—what it is best at, matched with what the world most wants it to deliver. The reason it's a big arrow that points up is because you always want to be pushing your resources and efforts in that direction. You should always be driving toward higher opportunity, higher capability. And we believe that if you hadn't previously been thinking this way about your business, this graph alone may be worth the price of this book.

Now imagine little arrows that are outside the big arrow. Anytime you have high opportunity and low capability or, conversely, great capability and very low opportunity, you shouldn't be pursuing that as a business. And had we had a tear-off copy of this graph in hand, perhaps Follywood—our movie site back on AOL in the early 1990s—would never have been born. Follywood was going to be a humorous and sarcastic look at Hollywood. And we were trying to do it at a time when you had to pay $3.50 an hour to use our site on AOL. Heck, how much did a movie cost to go see? Seven dollars. How much time did we need you, as our customer, to spend on our Follywood site to be profitable for that month? About ten hours. So we needed you to spend $35 reading our funny jokes about Hollywood when you were probably only going to spend $7 to $15 going to the movies that particular month. So, clearly we didn't think things through enough. When you're not playing your own game as a business you tend to make that mistake.

(On a side note, we also figured out over time that Americans don't really want jokes made about Hollywood. Most of us try to glamorize Hollywood. That's part of what it represents for us. We want movies to be big. We want people in the movies to be big.)

The sad thing about that for our business—and for any

business that makes this mistake—is that we paid an opportunity cost. The time and money we spent on that misguided little arrow could otherwise have been put toward bulking up a bigger and more relevant opportunity. Anyway, events like this can be good lessons, as long as they're not crippling. In our own case, we were young enough and small enough that we could blow it this way a few times and then finally learn the lesson. Larger, more mature businesses can't afford to make this mistake. They need the Big Arrow.

## THE INVESTING LESSON

Did we play someone else's game as investors? You betcha. So many of us did. Any investment of any consequence that was not socked into something with which you had an intimate familiarity, you weren't playing your game. Even if a few of those succeeded for you, they shouldn't have. It's a sucker's hope to strike it rich with the next spin of the roulette wheel. Picture that roulette wheel featuring, instead of numbers, names of public companies that sound "hot," though that's about the extent of your knowledge of them. Now spin that baby and pay thousands of dollars to drop a little ball onto it and "Round and round and round she goes, and where she stops NOBODY KNOWS."

Nobody. Particularly you . . . if you put yourself in this position.

Hey, the House probably wants you to win a few. That'll encourage you to come back for more . . . and, even after you begin your inevitable string of losses, to stay longer. Roulette wheel investing will do that to you.

One of our favorite stories, told in another Motley Fool book long ago, is so germane and so good that we're going to repeat it. (Those of you who remember this from *You Have More Than You Think*, clap along anyway.)

Fool HQ is located in Old Town Alexandria, Virginia, just across the river from our nation's capital. About a block from our building is a bar that, unfortunately, a number of our employees refer to as the employee lounge. (We're working on that with them.) So, um, we were there a while back, hanging out one Friday evening—sitting at a table with a guy next to us who was six foot five, dressed from head to toe in leather. (So you can see what kinds of bars we hang out in!) Okay, actually it was Memorial Day weekend, the weekend that motorcycle clubs ride on Capitol Hill to raise awareness about prisoners of war and those missing in action. So, our normally quaint and historic Old Town was for a brief time blanketed by leather and tattoos.

Anyway, he struck up a conversation: "What do you guys do?" And we began to talk about The Motley Fool and he said, "Investing. That's interesting. You know I only ever made one stock market investment, and my conclusion is that it's a great big gambling machine. A roulette wheel. I'm not willing to put the money that I've made into it. But lemme tell you about the one investment I made.

"I invested in a restaurant company that served breakfast in the Southeast. That was their primary business. And, I really didn't know anything about the company. I got a phone call from a broker in 1987 who said the market had crashed and this was actually a great time to invest. Prices are lower. You gotta lot of great businesses out there and let me tell you about this restaurant company." And he went on, "You know, I didn't know the broker at all. It was a phone call. Blind. But I did have some money saved so I took a few thousand dollars, five grand from my kid's college fund, and I invested it in the restaurant stock.

"The restaurant stock was trading in 1987 at $5 a share, so I guess I got a thousand shares. And now, ten years later it's still trading—you guys probably know this—it's trading on what are called the pink sheets. It's trading at about 25 cents a share. So, my five grand has been whittled all the way down to a few hundred bucks and I've come to the conclusion that the stock market is not the place for me to put my hard-earned savings. So guys, convince me."

So one of us (Tom, for the record) actually said to him, "Did you ever think about investing in Harley-Davidson?" And he punched Tom in the nose.

Okay, no, not quite—actually he perked up. "No, I didn't. Is Harley a company I can invest in?"

We said, "Actually, yes. Harley-Davidson has been an incredibly great company."

"I know. I ride Harleys."

So here was a guy who rode Harleys, surrounded for years by other people who rode Harleys. But when it came to investing his own life savings, he gave them to someone he didn't know, who did not have his best interests in mind, who put him in a company he wasn't familiar with. And his conclusion was that the stock market is a great big gambling machine.

We went back to our office after that conversation and typed in the numbers and Harley-Davidson is up more than 100 times in value since the October 1987 crash. So, his $5,000 would've turned into $500,000 if he'd bought what he knew, bought what he'd loved, bought what in many ways he was. Yet due to a widespread lack of financial education that is a shameful omission in this country's curriculum (and if you want to get The Motley Fool involved in helping out your neighborhood, district, school, state, nation, you can e-mail us at schoolsnow@Fool.com)—due to his lack of education, it simply had not occurred to him to align his savings with his knowledge base, to invest inside his circle of competence, to play his own game. He completely gave away home-field advantage.

Yet even as we're trying to teach this lesson, there we were two years ago with one of our real-money model portfolios at Fool.com investing in JDS Uniphase. Of all technology companies, one that was building optical networks using the speed of light to transfer data seemed like the best sort of future opportunity one could find. And truth be told the company's operational numbers did look great and the stock had responded for a few years, rising dozens of times in value. But if you're a stock market investor you probably know that onetime tech bellwether JDS Uniphase has since gone from

$140 to the single digits as of this writing at the end of 2001. The company has laid off half its staff and faces extreme difficulty.

So even as we're teaching the Harley lesson we must admit that if you dropped a heap of JDS Uniphase products in our lap—sans brand names—we would have real difficulty telling you what they were. Therefore, it behooves us to emphasize that each one of us has to learn and relearn this lesson throughout our lives—if we're not going to rely primarily on an index fund and some bond investments. Yep, no two ways around it: If we're going to make stock investments, they should be investments in companies with whose products and services we have the most familiarity.

Another way of putting this is simply to say that if we were handed a copy of your brokerage statement and invited to scan down your list of holdings, we should be able to tell a lot about you. It's just the same as when we visit your den (by the way, we're coming next Thursday just past noon), look over your library, peruse the titles therein, and wind up knowing a lot about *you*. Our books are our friends. They have been and are the intellectual company we keep; our personal shelves make known, even unintentionally, what we're interested in, and how we think about the world. And it should be exactly the same with your investment portfolio—your brokerage statement should afford an intimate look at you, not speaking of the amounts here, but rather the composition.

To close . . . does playing your own game mean you always win? Is it enough to be an enthusiast of Harley-Davidson and Starbucks and Gap and Boston Chicken—an authority on these companies—and therefore know that each will make you lots of money as an investor? Of course not (you may have noticed Boston Chicken's eventual bankruptcy). We're stating, no more and no less, that you must play your game in investing as in life. The only shares you should ever take in return for your money should come from companies whose products you truly understand and appreciate.

Judging from hundreds of discussions at book signings and speeches across the country for six years, and thousands of discussions online with people around the world for the past decade, many many many people haven't been playing their game—before the bear market, and in many cases through this bear market. Fortunately, tough times have caused many to look deeper, to reassess, to put some new standards in place, make new commitments. It is this new commitment you can make to yourself that will make a wonderful legacy as you—and one day your heirs—look back on these dark times and recognize what they did for your character, and your bottom line.

# 3

# We Didn't Respect Profitability . . . Enough

Supporting any business that you run, work for, or invest in is its business model. Unfortunately for many of us, business models are rarely taught outside business schools. Consequently, many who go on to work for businesses as adults lack a basic knowledge or appreciation of business models in general, sometimes their own company's business model in particular. Intellectually curious types try to pick up the stuff as they go along. To speed your progress, a very fine primer on business models for non–MBA students is *The Profit Zone*, by Adrian Slywotzky and David Morrison.

The phrase "business model" itself masks a simpler expression of the concept: how people make profits. Simply stated, lemonade stands generate revenues through sales of lemonade, and they earn profits by selling that lemonade for more than it costs to produce. Is this the business model? Not exactly. Business models involve a richer, more thoroughgoing explanation of how people make the profits. For instance, one lemonade stand's business model might involve consistent positioning at a town's most trafficked intersections, moving around based on the time of day. Another's may heavily rely on repeat business by emphasizing that it has the best-tasting lemonade, encouraging referrals. Another stand may inject caffeine into its drink, addicting its customers. (Oh wait, sorry, that's Coca-Cola's business model.) Another may do all three of the things listed above: Starbucks.

One principle that seemed to get lost in the race for prosperity at the end of the 1990s was the quality and plausibility of the business model, a true focus on profitability. As we look back at what happened in preparation for our next section, What to Do Now, mistake number three is that we didn't respect profitability . . . enough.

## THE BUSINESS LESSON

Our own business in the late 1990s did not have a true business model, beyond the goal of maximizing audience to earn advertising dollars. But we did have a strategy. And earlier, we shared a key component of that business strategy: It's what we'll call here "planned burn." We were raising money to spend that money, after which we were going to raise more money to spend more money—returning to profitability of course, we hoped. And in the meantime getting really, really big! That was our plan. Of course, we were like many young companies who need early money to grow, just as a small green shoot can't survive without external help like rain and sun. Plants have nature; companies have venture capitalists. It is only the very rare company that can be profitable right away off of a shoelace or, in the case of eBay, off of a PEZ dispenser.

By the way, even eBay took venture capital (we share the same financier with them, in fact, Seattle-based Maveron Fund).

Yes, very, very few businesses can achieve any significant scale early without giving part ownership away to venture capitalists in return for a few hundred thousand or a few million dollars.

The critical point comes when you ask yourself, "Having accepted this first investment, do we want a second one? And if so, how much can we realistically expect to raise?" If you are going to burn through your next round—that is, intentionally overspend your means in hopes of growing to a scale sufficient to achieve sustainable profitability—then be clear on what business model you're burning toward. In our own experience and from our observations, we conclude that many entrepreneurs and business managers can get too focused on financing and not enough on the blocking and tackling necessary to turn a profit. Sometimes outside observers can see that better about your business than you can. It's a great argument for setting up a board of outside directors.

It wasn't until 1999—six years into our business—that we seriously began to ask ourselves, Who is our customer? Ostensibly, our customer was the reader of our Web site. But for any free service on the Web, or off, that hopes to profit from advertising reach, your customer is actually your sponsor paying money to keep the site free! Again, when you run a free advertising Web site, it's easy to believe that the customer is the person who taps into your site. But it's just not true. The simplest, best definition of "customer" is "the one who pays for a product or service." And indeed, most media companies are similar to The Motley Fool in that when they are broadcasting on television or elsewhere, their customer is also the advertiser. Perhaps we're sharing a commonplace—perhaps you realized this already and so no great business insight here—but we only came to this realization after six years of doing business in our own space. So part of respecting profitability is having a very clear idea of exactly what you're doing.

When you really think it through this way you come to find that the customer base of any media company, that is, the audience of advertising-based content, is the product! That product, the audience, is being served up to advertisers, the customers—whether we're talking network TV, radio, many magazines, or most Web sites.

Anyway, one thing we've been doing over the past few years is transitioning to get more direct payments from our audience, which we do hope will prove more satisfying to all involved. Anybody who is a member of our audience in one or another context or medium would, we hope, be comforted to discover that via direct payments they're now our customer as opposed to being our product. This allows us a great opportunity to serve both our customers—advertisers and audience. Our advertisers are given a place to show off their new services designed to benefit our audience—individual investors.

So there's a media company view of the world. And yet again, as a mostly media company, it took us year number six in our nine years of business before we understood and came to grips with that. In fact, most of this realization occurred because all of a sudden advertising began to dry up—it took some of the darkest economic years in the past century to whack this through our thick skulls. We gained a deeper respect and a healthier appreciation for profitability.

Now there are a lot of people, some of them quite well known in business, who don't respect profitability very much. Yesterday's expensive office space taken out by many fledgling companies is now, just a few years later, the stuff of business cliché. These companies certainly hadn't "earned" the rights to such luxury, beyond just their ability to raise lots of money. (Indeed, does a truly good business ever bask in such luxury, when that money could instead have been paid out as a dividend to shareholders?) The Internet bust that followed turned many of these grand palaces of indulgence into what industry observers now term "see-through buildings."

In the fall of 2001, the *San Jose Mercury News* reported the highest vacancy rates in modern Silicon Valley history. See-through buildings dotted the landscape due to their owners or tenants being unable, halfway through construction, to afford ceilings or interior walls. The *Merc* reported, "Redback Networks, whose stock has plummeted from $191 a share last spring to $1.20, has a see-through building in North San Jose. It's so empty that motorists heading west on Highway 237 have a clear view through the tinted green glass to the field on the other side." There were so many properties on the market at the time that landlords and brokers were "offering incentives, not just to agents who snag tenants, but to agents who simply attend an open house and tour a location."

A clear sign of a troubled business is one with numerous, undisciplined costs. These provide an easy tip-off, no? They wear their gaudy hearts on their sleeve (presuming hearts can be described as gaudy). The manager cannot control his desire to spend spend spend, and this is quite evident in the office location, the office furniture, the "special effects" (we kid you not, we toured a failed Internet company's building in Atlanta and they had all sorts of cool mauve stagelights, funkadelic decor, and plans for a large outdoor theater up on the roof of their complex—and we were wondering who was paying for this stuff!). Perchance you know someone like this. Say, someone like Donald Trump.

In fact, we had the pleasure of sitting opposite The Donald in his offices a few years ago. In our portfolio we were short his stock, Trump Hotels & Casino Resorts (for noninvestor types, "short" means we were betting against Donald's stock— you can read more about shorting in *The Motley Fool Investment Guide*). And because we pick stocks totally out in the open at The Motley Fool, everyone knew it. And in time, The Donald came to know it too. And so he wanted to talk to us.

This occasioned some anxiety at Fool HQ.

In fact, pulling a page from what Iraq did to a personal friend of ours named Tom Ewald a decade ago, we decided that the best way to approach this meeting was to take along a human shield. And so we actually took one of our summer interns with us—one of the sweetest people you'll ever meet, a young woman named Charity.

She had come to us from the University of North Carolina. She was probably nineteen. She had never been to New York City before. In fact, she told us she had never been on a plane before! So Charity graciously agreed to go on a plane with us to New York City, thence straight to the top floor of Trump Tower to Donald Trump's personal headquarters.

We were greeted in the lobby by his then CEO. Now, if Donald was the Wicked Witch of the West, this fellow was one of the flying monkeys. Actually, he couldn't have been a more gracious man, but he also couldn't have been more of a puppet. "Donald is waiting for you," he intoned, and we pro-

ceeded inside to the gilt chamber of The Donald, seated behind a massive mahogany desk.

When we talk in this chapter about not respecting profitability, Trump Hotels & Casino Resorts makes an apt poster
child. Trump's private company, his real estate company, is
profitable and very well regarded, often listed as one of the
top ten in the United States of America. On the other hand, his
public company—representing his casinos and resorts—has a
record of dramatic unprofitability. Here's how it happened:
Trump took the Trump Marina, a property that he owned in
his private real estate company, and sold it at an exorbitant
price to his public company. His public company had to borrow a billion dollars to make the purchase. And ever since,
with expensive break-even operations, the company has been
whacked by the interest payments it must make, year in and
year out. The stock fell from a high of $35 some years ago to
$4.86 where we shorted it.

For good reasons. Please note that from the standpoint of
his private company, this was a brilliant strategy, as with one
swell foop it was rewarded with immediate profits due to the
overinflated sale. From the standpoint of his public company,
it was a killing move—Trump left his shareholders, including
many institutions and members of the general public, saddled
with an overpriced property that weighed like a millstone
around the company's breast.

If you're interested in reading more of a blow-by-blow de-
scription of The Motley Fool meets Donald Trump, tap into
Fool.com and search the site for our article, "I Own the Water,"
because that's exactly what The Donald said to us when we
talked about Trump Marina. (We can still picture Charity lean-
ing as far back in her chair—away from him—as she could.)
Not long after meeting him, we cashed out of our short—quite
profitably, we might add—taking him at his word at the time
that the company would restructure its debt and go on to succeed. Last we looked, the debt situation looked the same; the
stock was below $2. We don't expect that one ever to come
back.

Which is often what eventually happens when you're working for or invested in a business whose primary focus is any-thing but profitability. Self-aggrandizement isn't designed to make others rich, and no surprise how often a situation like The Donald's is the result.

To close this portion of the lesson, then, let it be said that there are a lot of people who don't respect profitability, some of whom are even considered quite successful over short pe-riods of time. But it's not a business lesson to study unless you're studying failure in order to avoid it. As businessmen, we have certainly gained a greater—and healthier—respect for profitability, and all that it comes to demand of you and your business. The lessons have been heartbreaking, especially as it became clear to us that we had overhired by a factor of sev-eral times above the level that our business would profitably support. And thus our company bid goodbye to so many good people in the year of 2001. It is to them that this book is ded-icated.


## THE INVESTING LESSON

The more one invests, the further one learns to look past Wall Street buy ratings, whisper numbers, and whether for a given quarter a company's earnings of 7 cents per share were a penny above or below estimates.

The more one invests, the more one comes to appreciate, even to love, the business model of what you're investing in. More time spent understanding how a company makes money—and how it plans to make more money than that—equates to a greater appreciation for the foundations of a busi-ness and its long-term possibilities. That, in turn, relates directly to your own chances of making money on the invest-ment.

The contrasting pasts of eBay and Amazon.com, both high-profile players during the Internet boom, are made evident by their respective business models.

eBay has been profitable from the day they went into business; Amazon.com, until just last quarter, finally, was best described as "no profit, all burn." (Perhaps it is noteworthy that, though they are both Internet-based retail businesses, Amazon's corporate name has always sported "dot-com" while eBay's hasn't needed to?) Despite this important contrast, for their first few years on the public markets, Amazon.com sported a significantly higher price tag. Its brand, its reach, its popularity, and its frequent likening to a "new Wal-Mart" held far more sex appeal than eBay's comparatively "niche" (this was the thinking at the time) positioning for traders of collectibles. A twenty-four-hour garage sale around the world didn't fly with enough investors compared to "Earth's Biggest Bookstore." Probably Amazon's more traditional and therefore graspable business model of straight retail seemed like easier money.

But again, think about that. In a topsy-turvy market that was failing to respect profitability enough, cash-burner Amazon .com achieved a much higher market capitalization than profitable sister eBay. And it was Amazon.com CEO Jeffrey Bezos, not eBay's CEO Meg Whitman, who earned *Time*'s "Man of the Year" designation for 1999. Perhaps Bezos's decision to leave Wall Street for dot-comdom played bigger as a story than eBay's birth.

eBay came about when the girlfriend (and now wife) of the founder turned to him and said, "Pierre, you know I have these PEZ dispensers in my attic and some people collect these things. You're always on the Internet. Could you list them there for sale?" (Not much retail of any kind was transacted online, back then.) So he listed them locally and they sold in a day. They went back up to the attic and found a few more things and listed those, and they sold too. And so literally from the first transaction, eBay has been profitable. But perhaps because of its founders' serendipity, its silliness, or comparative lack of professionalism, the story of eBay's founding didn't suggest "big opportunity" in the same way that choosing the name "Amazon" and sticking it together with "dot-com" did for Bezos. Thus, despite losing money (purposefully planned burn) hand over fist for years, Amazon carried a higher company value than the little PEZ dispenser that could.

Now we're seeing the fallout of those two models. As of this writing, eBay is valued at $15 billion, its stock having risen 22 percent in the past twelve months. Amazon.com, on the other hand, is today valued at just $4.7 billion, one third the value of eBay. Step back and look at how the Internet has shaped up, realizing that the same truth applies to just about any other industry that matures: In the end, really only a handful of sustainable success stories emerge in any boom era. And those companies are almost always the ones that really valued business profits enough, and the resulting cash in hand. They usually didn't succeed with a model based on burn. Amazon.com may still succeed—and one of us remains invested in it—but that's a big question that remains very much up in the air, whereas eBay has it made in the shade.

Please note that burn models can succeed. *USA Today* was not profitable for the first decade of its operations and was mocked as "McPaper." But now McPaper is ubiquitous, from dispensing machines to hotel doormats, and about as profitable as McDonald's to boot. Among many others, MTV featured an extended planned burn model as well. But the primary point remains that we investors are speculating when we invest in public companies that are still working through planned burn, and for this reason such stakes should constitute small portions of our portfolios. One must at least recognize Peter Lynch's advice to just cross off your list all companies that are losing money.

Next chapter we'll point to a key example of one company that was losing money when we invested in it. So one can turn an occasional blind eye on Lynch's dictum, but should always do so knowingly, well aware that speculation more frequently leads to losses, and often greater losses, at that. The problem with the past five years is that so many of us were turning a blind eye, but didn't think we were blind. This or that company would "ultimately come to dominate all health care online," game over, concede them their (unearned) billions. This other thing will dominate the sale of music. Remember K-Tel? We hope not. But if you do, you'll first remember K-Tel albums from the 1970s. You saw them directly marketed on TV ads for *K-Tel's Greatest Hits* albums and whatnot. And then out of the blue K-Tel announced in 1998, "We're an Internet retailer also." And this was a $6 stock that went to $44 over the next two weeks. And then over the next three years it went from $67 to less than a dollar. So they created a lot of brief excitement by saying, "Me too—we're associated with this great boom also." But they weren't profitable and there was no cash for them to expand. So we go back to Standard Oil and Rockefeller and say he was right: The competitive battles in the business world are won by the companies who are able to store up cash and continue to operate profitably over time. And if you tend to make most or all of your investment dollars flow their way over time, as an investor you'll win right along with them.

A lot of companies that went public over the last five years didn't operate from that philosophy. They couldn't! They weren't profitable in the first place, and didn't have a plausible business model with clearly visible profitability, anyway.

# 4

# We
# Pursued Growth
# at Any Cost

We've already taken a look at see-through buildings, which also double as a symbolic embodiment of growth pursued at any cost. Growth pursued at any cost leads to eventual impoverishment.

## THE BUSINESS LESSON

When Enron failed and garnered most of the biggest bear market headlines, it took some of the attention away from other behemoths that had hugely swooned. Lucent Technologies rose spectacularly throughout the mid-1990s and then imploded even more spectacularly as the economy slowed and eventually slipped into recession. Lucent pursued policies of aggressive growth later shown to be growth at any cost. How was this manifest? And could you have seen this coming?

Lucent, the maker of telecommunications and networking equipment, overstuffed its retail channels with Lucent products. The company's large and successful presence in the marketplace notwithstanding, Lucent wound up creating far more stuff than their customers desired or could afford, meaning in effect that lots of Lucent equipment was sitting on the shelves.

Via a process called "channel stuffing," Lucent could show that sales and profits had been generated—selling their products to middlemen—when in fact the middlemen couldn't sell the stuff and would later return it to Lucent. Further, the company provided extremely generous financing terms to its customers, enabling them to "purchase" Lucent equipment—"purchase" in quotes since who was really paying for these products? There's an unfortunately large discrepancy between sales booked on a company's income statement and real sales, for which a company is fully paid. Beware companies that aggressively finance their own sales.

Lucent's ratio of growth in accounts receivable (that is, booked sales that have not yet been paid with cash) to growth in revenues was constantly rising from 1997 on. There were clear warning signs of what might and eventually did happen. Any reader of our Fool.com online service watched this unfold with a knowledgeable eye, particularly given our ongoing published observations that the company's Foolish Flow Ratio (covered in our *Motley Fool Investment Guide,* but for the financially inclined it's the sum of current assets minus cash divided by the sum of current liabilities minus short-term debt) had been rising for an amazing eleven consecutive quarters. This indicated that Lucent was shelling out a lot of extra cash to pay for its current assets, assets like inventory and uncollected payments from customers. Not good.

And why? Lucent management, particularly the egregiously bad CEO Richard McGinn, had led Wall Street toward predictions of high growth rates in sales and earnings. That put pressure on the company to consistently deliver (or at least temporarily pretend to deliver) what it had said it would. Unfortunately for all concerned, management could not own up to this reality, obscuring its financial problems behind labyrinthine financial statements. As The Motley Fool's senior analyst Bill Mann stated, "I once tried to work through Lucent's financials and found the same thing: Tables that crossed over to other tables, contradictory statements, vague references, and other things that did nothing to help investors understand the company. The only enlightenment I gained from the experience was that such reporting would be a great way for a company to hide something."

These are the desperate measures employed by those who pursue growth at any cost—particularly the cost of a company's future. What McGinn and his team did to Lucent is the corporate equivalent of a new president secretly tripling government spending off a diminished tax base and then hiding all of that for a sustained period until some journalist begins to find out—and then disappearing before the next election, leaving his successors to deal with the consequences.

Lucent is a classic example of the pursuit of growth at any cost: overstuffed inventory channels brimming with unfairly booked sales, financing extended to people who otherwise wouldn't have bought the product and in many cases never finally paid for it anyway. That this occurred on such a grand scale and that few were able to piece it together early enough is astonishing. That Enron would do many of the same things on an even bigger scale two years later must, we suppose, be less astonishing—since we already should have learned from Lucent and Nortel Networks and JDS Uniphase et al. that anything can happen in today's business world, and the bigger they come the harder they fall.

The best way to pursue growth is with careful planning and dependable numbers, and at a cost people understand: aka cash that you already have in the bank. Planned growth from existing resources need not be slow growth, either. When we think of a company that does that right we think of Starbucks. Starbucks on the face of it has grown crazily, insanely—its stores seem to multiply like rabbits. In Vancouver, British Columbia, there are several places where there are two or more Starbucks stores on the same block, some even at the same intersection! The company seems to have discovered that the more Starbucks you populate an area with, the better each one does. Some weird new coffee networking effect? Perhaps. It is worthwhile to note, in passing, that consumer-facing businesses rarely can hide their performance and their financial reporting as easily or long as business-to-business players like Lucent.

Starbucks management has consistently made their growth measured growth, clearly outlining their plans for such-and-such thousand stores built by such-and-such year. And then doing it. The projections are often aggressive, but never involve cash or resources that the company cannot clearly afford. Starbucks's growth is not growth at any cost, but rather at a manageable cost, one that has enabled the company to be consistently and increasingly profitable over the past decade. In fact, Starbucks shareholders (including David, as of this writing) should have reacted proudly to a joke put out a while ago by *The Onion,* the online humor site. It said, "Starbucks has a new growth strategy. They're opening up a new Starbucks in the men's room of an existing Starbucks." We want jokes like that to be made about each company we're invested in; the more your company can break into pop culture for reasons surrounding its products, name, or growth, the better. (To say nothing of the Starbucks that headquarters Dr. Evil's empire in *Austin Powers: The Spy Who Shagged Me.*)

In this way, Starbucks functions as the corporate opposite of Lucent, two completely different pursuits of growth. Which one is taking place at your company?

## THE INVESTING LESSON

Pursuing growth at any cost as investors means eschewing valuation.

That's been a very dangerous game played by investors over the last couple of years and we ourselves have played it to an extent, believing valuation work to be overrated. Here's why we thought that, and the lesson we've learned over the last twenty-four months.

For us as long-term investors, our argument has gone, It's better to overpay for a great company that will trounce its competitors and dominate its markets than to invest in lesser companies. Because we've focused so much on great companies, and because they're traditionally so "overvalued"-looking and yet still go on to beat the market averages anyway, we have logically tsk-tsked the use of traditional valuation metrics in such situations. If you were hoping to buy Microsoft at a price-to-earnings ratio of 12, you would never ever have gotten near buying one of the great stocks of the past twenty years. Etcetera.

This isn't to say we pay no attention to valuation at all. We won't pay the equivalent of a thousand dollars for a Barbie doll. But we will pay up to twice what the doll is worth if we're planning on holding the investment for a long time, because we believe over that time the company will outperform all others in its industry. Patience.

Two companies in particular have proven highly influential to us over the course of our investing careers. These companies have defied all the so-called value investors (people who invest their dollars in stocks they believe to be undervalued, often companies that are overlooked or depressed). They have done this on their way to some of the best returns available on the public markets over the past decade and more. Yet we have based perhaps too much of our investment approach on such companies.

The first is General Electric. If you are serious about business or investing and have not picked up *Straight from the Gut* by Jack Welch (and John A. Byrne), it's a wonderful book just released late last year. To paraphrase a great Welch point of the past: I don't think my stock can ever get overvalued. Let me explain why. My whole modus operandi, my whole business approach is to hire the greatest managers and train them and make sure that I have the best managers in all of business. And that means that if my stock gets above what I think the fair value is, I will use that currency to buy a company with lesser skills at the management level and install my managers, thereby increasing the value of General Electric. That's my business plan. It's worked for me for twenty years and that's how I believe General Electric will continue to expand in value even if you think our multiple was too high.

But again, it's dangerous to predicate your investment approach on an assumption that every company has America's greatest CEO over the past fifty years. There's only one Jack

Welch. And GE with a market cap of $390 billion and a high price-to-earnings ratio, which makes the stock look consistently overpriced, is largely a reflection of its great management. So what is true for General Electric is not something that you can apply casually to any other company. Most other companies are not saying, "We spend a lot of time training our managers." Rather, too many spend their time saying, "We're going to beat our quarterly numbers," or, "We feel good about a new product that we have out." They're not saying or thinking, "Over the next quarter century, we're going to build an institution."

And yet with some of our other companies, we often thought they were. Because its financial statements looked like a mini-GE, a small dynamo ready to spit fire in every competitive direction, we ascribed to Yahoo! the same mind-set as Jack Welch. (The numbers looked just as good!) But the reality is that if you base your conviction on every company having a Jack Welch and thinking like Jack Welch, maybe you would pay the same premium to own their stock. But every company does not. Which means you have to look more skeptically at the valuation of even a very profitable and promising (at least at the time, and in some ways still) Yahoo! Maybe like GE it could for a while, but now with its market cap down to $11 billion, Yahoo! can no longer use its stock like currency. It's not as easy for it to find great people as it is for General Electric. And great people are what most significantly and surely expand a business over time.

The second company that tricked us was America Online.

We first invested back in 1994, when we were privileged to read voraciously and thoroughly our own online community's debate about AOL stock on our site's discussion boards. We had been using the service for ourselves for four years. The company had been public for only about two years, and was only just gaining greater momentum than Prodigy and CompuServe (its early competitors—remember those days?). Our discussion group, involving thousands of contributors over the course of many moons, debated vibrantly and memorably over just what the heck this company was about, and where it was going. If you've been out in our discussion groups you know they can sometimes get heated, and let us say that there was a lot of heat there, particularly early on. The debate was over whether AOL would ever be profitable! AOL was still burning through what would end up being some $360 million of marketing, sending all of us six to eight to ten to twelve different AOL discs, which at least one cocktail party we heard of used as coasters. It almost appeared absurd. Almost. Numerous articles and opinions in the financial press were extremely critical of AOL, as were various members of the Fool community, who were saying:

"This thing is outrageously overvalued."

"This company hasn't even turned a profit."

Once it did, "It's trading at 500 times earnings!"

In their minds, AOL would never be able to justify the price tag being applied to it.

In the face of all that, we bought. For the next two consecutive summers, AOL stock would be called "the most overvalued stock in America" by a large and well-publicized meeting of money managers. You know the rest of the story. Up a few hundred times in value from there. And we continue to hold it to this day.

So is this a Motley Fool bragfest? Are we taking up your valuable time to puff out our feathered bellies and jut out our beaks? No. We're explaining an investment mistake we've been making.

The point here is that we had found a company called America Online the very decade that America was going online. Now ask yourself how often such situations occur. And keep asking. Because strong companies in perfect positions to expand massively into huge and relevant industries over short periods of time just do not come along very often. So again, while this company may enjoy a valuation that appeared to be huge (and hugely unjustified to many at the time), that doesn't mean that every other growth company that appears poised to lead its industry deserves a similar premium.

Hey, we were holding shares of a business that nobody seemed able to value! Some analysts on Wall Street were putting price tags of $250 a share on the stock at the same time that others were slapping on targets of $3 a share. And $250 was way too low! There was a huge short interest (again, investment bets placed in belief that a stock will fall). Anyway, now we can wrap these two together.

We took the valuations of these two companies, a GE driven by an ever-ascending model of great management together with an America Online that would prove America's most enduring great growth stock of the 1990s, and we began to apply those lessons to other investments that looked to hold significant promise. Back to Yahoo! Yahoo! at its peak had 30 percent net profit margins; it was making 30 cents on every dollar of sales. It looked like a baby GE, a baby Microsoft, until you stepped back and realized how cyclical advertising can be, and (more important) how the Internet really is more a direct marketing medium, at a time when Yahoo! was relying on (indirect) banner ads. Yahoo! had neither prepared for that, nor was its stock being priced in consideration of that. Anyway, their operational and business ratios on paper looked as good as those of AOL and GE so that even when our investment ran up to $208 a share, we just kept holding on. Everything was okay! We were pretty darn happy! And they may use that stock to acquire other companies (that turned out to be similarly inflated), so don't worry about actually valuing the business . . .

It became clear over the succeeding 1,000-, 2,000-, 3,000-point drop in the value of the Nasdaq that learning how to value a business is important. Eschewing valuation by knocking it off your list and saying, "This is a great company like AOL and GE!"—pursuing growth at any cost—is not a dependable way to beat the stock market averages over time. Unless you can rely on finding one or two or three great companies that allow you to cross out a lot of mistakes, we suggest you do go out and accomplish the work of determining ballpark numbers for how much a business would be worth if another company were to acquire it.

What approaches do we use? The very ones we taught in our *Motley Fool Investment Guide*. It's not that we didn't believe in those; it's that we didn't use them as much in our quest for the Great Company. Let us make it clear as we close that we continue to focus on company quality over low valuation. But we don't skip doing the valuing, especially after a stock we've bought continues to go up, way up, afterward. We don't "buy and hold," we "buy to hold," hoping we'll get to hold for a long time. But we'd be richer Fools today if we had sold some past mega-winners at a high multiple of where those shares eventually fell a few years later. The irony in those cases is that, often, business quality didn't diminish. The companies in many cases only got better at what they were doing in operations. The primary factor that did change was the marketplace's way of valuing those companies, and as the stocks fell—in some cases dramatically—we lost out through our decisions to ignore their valuation, to reject it as unimportant.

So as to not ignore valuation, you can learn more on how to value shares of a company through our series of articles online at Fool.com/school/howtovaluestocks.htm.

Let us not pursue growth at any cost.

# 5

# We Failed
# to Recognize
# Our Errors

Given that the previous four chapters elucidate four mistakes that we and perhaps many others made over the previous several years, it's logical to conclude with this fifth key mistake: allowing your errors to persist. It's easy to see in retrospect and yet harder to do in the heat of battle, but the successful person in business and investing can recognize his errors either as he's making them or shortly thereafter. How? Would that a fail-safe approach existed, but in our experience some mixture of the following ingredients helps: humility, open-mindedness, good listening skills, and a willingness to see things as they are, not as you would wish them to be.

Failing to recognize one's errors compounds them.

Consider the Mars Climate Orbiter. Early on the morning of September 23, 1999, the orbiter fired its main engine and five minutes later the spacecraft passed behind Mars (as seen from Earth), as planned. But the orbiter never emerged around the other side, leaving NASA and its California-based Jet Propulsion Laboratory with a sad, expensive, and embarrassing loss.

What happened? A NASA spokesman the next day stated, "We don't know."

One week later, an internal review team recognized the problem as failed communication between the spacecraft team in Colorado and the navigation team in California. Ay, here was the rub: "The peer review preliminary findings indicate that one team used English units (e.g., inches, feet, and pounds) while the other used metric units for a key spacecraft operation." No joke. Consequently, the craft flew too low in the Martian atmosphere, burned, and crashed on the Martian surface. At a cost of $125 million.

A statement by Dr. Edward Weiler, NASA's then Associate Administrator for Space Science, began, "People sometimes make errors." Which is absolutely regrettable and absolutely true. However, Weiler went on to say, "The problem here was not the error, it was the failure of NASA's systems engineering, and the checks and balances in our processes to detect the error. That's why we lost the spacecraft."

In other words, even more than a technology problem or a worker bee problem, NASA had a managerial problem. An expensive one. NASA had failed to recognize its own errors, and look at the result.

Two months later the Climate Orbiter's sister aircraft, the Mars Polar Lander, was about 100 feet over the planet and preparing to land. Its lander legs deployed and a software error told the engines to shut down. One hundred feet too soon.

CRASH!

A crash costing in excess of $150 million. What a mission!

The NASA blue ribbon report findings on that one? There had been a full-scale test of the suspect software before flight, but some touchdown sensors were incorrectly wired. After the wiring was corrected, the test had not been repeated. "Had the defect been known," a spokesman noted, "a software correction would have been simple and inexpensive."

The two fatal plunges into the Red Planet in the autumn of 1999 cost American taxpayers a total of more than $300 million.

Did we have to go a million miles away and eat $300 million to make our point? Probably not. So, from Mars to your armchair . . .

## THE BUSINESS LESSON

Most business mistakes are failures to adapt to customer needs. Perhaps the business didn't recognize those needs, or maybe didn't prepare its internal processes to deliver to those needs. What have you. The result is that business—which is just a highfalutin term for the simple act of getting paid for satisfying customer needs—didn't happen in sufficient volume or sufficient time. The competition won—or if there was no meaningful competition, then customers walked away empty.

Our book *Rule Breakers, Rule Makers* first presented our comparison of the process of business to the process of scientific evolution. If you warm to our viewpoint, you will quickly see that a critical piece of business acumen—what you'll want to inject into the DNA of your business—is the ability to adapt to changes in external circumstances. These circumstances are often beyond our control in the same way that the Ice Age was beyond mortal control. In business, we mustn't spend time cursing the coming Ice Age, or pretending it might not occur—we just adapt. Immediately. And as thoroughly as possible. Survival depends on it, and the businesses that do survive are the ones that will pass their genes (and their version of history) on to the next generation. Those that do not are like Ogg, the Ice Age caveman who refused to migrate to warmer climes. (Which is why you've never heard of him.)

Seen through the lens of evolution, the failure to recognize one's errors—our subject this chapter—is simply a failure of adaptation. The world changed, an organization didn't change with it. The responsibility is therefore always squarely with you the manager. Either management failed to foresee the changing circumstances, or instead did, and did not effectively adapt to them.

Business is evolution. The process of natural selection that occurs in nature occurs in business as well—the natural selection being done by customers of businesses. Customers select and therefore determine survival, which is why knowing your customer and her reasons for selecting is so important. And why keeping her satisfied enough to stay with you through thick and through thin is so important. As Harry Beckwith, author of the excellent *Selling the Invisible,* has written:

> Any failing of your service should not be ignored or hidden. You should take the hit right away, fix the problem, and in so doing let your customer know that "You really matter to us, and we will get this right for you." Big mistakes are big opportunities.

Beckwith is saying, "Don't fail to recognize your errors"—our mantra this chapter. Actually, he's saying more than that. He's saying that your errors are catalysts to take action. They are opportunities to be exploited.

One superior marketing consultant who visited us at Fool HQ concurs. Speaking of customer complaints and how to approach them, he called them "complaint discoveries." Those two words epitomize our point.

Discover complaints. Then turn those discoveries into discoveries. Then: Adapt.


## THE INVESTING LESSON

Many of us will be cursed all our lives long with making the same investing mistakes over and over again. Or it'll seem that way.

Here's why.

Everything that goes wrong can later be blamed on one or another example of poor thinking. That's a given. The problem is that examples of poor thinking are so numerous that many of them contradict each other, seemingly total opposites! So if you recognize you blew it, decide it's because you did such-and-such thing, and then next time do the exact opposite, you can get into as much or more trouble that way. And then if your resulting conclusion is that you went the wrong direction that second time and should just do the opposite of that, you're back to mistake number one again. Rinse and repeat, for decades.

An example. Many will decide they were taking too much risk with their investments throughout the great investing years of 1995–99. So, having only recently recognized and admitted that error (graduating from the school of hard knocks), they will go on to take much less risk. And some will eventually conclude, looking over their brokerage statements years hence, that they overreacted and failed to take enough risk. Consider that some of those same people were taking too little risk prior to 1995, which is why they finally decided to buy some risky "tech stocks" sometime around 1999. And so on, and so on.

Here is the right way to think about this. Do not spend time bouncing from one extreme to the other, skipping up and down the spectrum at the speed of light. Instead, search for what Aristotle called the Golden Mean. He phrased it thus: "Moral virtue is a mean between two extremes, the one involving excess and the other deficiency." Let's put that fundamental approach to living in investment terms: "Good investing is a mean between two extremes, the one involving greed and the other fear." Constantly calibrating and recalibrating your risks is a never-ending labor for the committed investor. If fear you must, make it a greedy fear. Conversely, any greedy thoughts you have should be leavened with whatever fear you can muster.

Done properly, you'll recognize your errors as an investor and, importantly, go on to address them appropriately. That will mean cutting a steadier course down the middle, neither expecting good weather to last forever nor quitting altogether with a storm on the horizon.

Yes, the process of making mistakes, recognizing them, and then addressing them continues throughout our lives. This fifth lesson from the great boom of the 1990s is the most timeless of all. Even Alan Greenspan's storied run as the Fed chief was marred by numerous key errors when he failed to lower interest rates in late 2000, pushing the economy into recession. With pundits insisting the Fed must ease the flow of money or risk crushing an already weakening economy, Greenspan and his merry band did nothing in December. Lo and behold on January 3, 2001, the Fed moved outside of its normal meeting schedule to slash the federal funds rate by half a percent, the largest single slash since 1992. The stock market within minutes rose an incredible 11 percent, a reaction showing the desperation of the situation, as desperate as the Fed's own rare move to act on interest rates outside of its normal Federal Open Market Committee meetings. The Fed was owning up to a mistake.

And, astonishingly, the committee did this again just a few months later.

Now two intermeeting interest rate cuts are so unusual that we may arrive at one primary conclusion: namely, the committee screwed up royally by not easing money beginning in the fourth quarter of 2000 to create the true "soft landing" economists were hoping for. Instead, the Fed acted late, twice, off schedule, and by the time the smoke had cleared in 2001, the Fed still scrambling and reeling, interest rates had been lowered an incredible eleven consecutive times.

Should we end this chapter by holding up Greenspan Inc. as a NASA-like repeat offender of failing to recognize one's errors? Or do we give this chapter a happy ending by pointing out the unusual measures the Fed subsequently took to shore up a battered economy? We'll allow you—or history—to write the ending. The lesson is concluded.

The markets are down. The economy has absorbed a staggering number of layoffs, and our nation has undergone a forced transformation into a security-conscious, but less-efficient place to do business and to live. Out of necessity. Two horrendous consecutive years of bad economic numbers and worse stock market returns. We have finished reflecting, and we have learned from the recent past now concluded.

We will not be impatient.

We will play our game.

We will give profitability its due respect.
We will not pursue growth at any cost.
And we will recognize and correct our own errors.

Indeed, all that matters now is the future.

It's time for What to Do Now.

# PART TWO

# WHAT
# TO DO NOW

Once you begin to believe there is help out there,
you will know it to be true.

— SAINT BARTHOLOMEW

What are we to do now with our finances? Corporate earnings have collapsed. More than a million jobs were cut in the
past two years. The broader stock market indices have all
fallen more than 20 percent from their highs. Hundreds of
IPOs from the 1990s are now demoralized or defunct
businesses. And investors are looking at retirement
portfolios down 20 percent to 50 percent.

Not just a few of us are concerned. We who may,
a few years ago, have whiled away afternoons with a

whiskery strand of long grass 'tween our teeth, chasing but-
terflies among the buttercups (or mayhap we sat around
playing Nintendo), without a financial care, we are now a
little bit worried. Gone are the rising salary checks, the
vanishing bills, gone the hallway high-fives from the boss,
gone the years when Cisco doubled and split, then doubled.
And now our collective prospect of owning that three-
floor beachhouse overlooking the Gulf of Mexico and throw
in the ski cottage in Jackson Hole, while giving liberally to
charities in addition to funding little Jim's and Janey's college educations four times over, are gone. So many of our
hopes, so much of our pride, beaten like flowers bent in the
rain.

What now?

Most of the answers are, in fact, relatively easy; some are
maddeningly complex. But the first best step in financial
planning in any circumstance is simply to reflect. Always. Not
options trading. Nor buying on dips. Nor hoarding cash.
Neither emotion nor action nor anything but reflection. Days
of it, if necessary. If you've come into an inheritance or a
huge salary bonus, then—for days and days, if you need it—
reflect. If you've just lost your job or now find your stock
portfolio in tatters, then stand apart from it and reflect. Even
if bankruptcy is throwing boots at your head, stop and
think.

It may sound simple. It isn't. Hasty thought and action are
extremely tempting. We want to stay on the move. That way
we're protected from having to review our past, accept our
faults, and learn. Yet sadly, all this unconsidered action can
ruin us financially. Mixing impatience with financial concern is
something like stirring arsenic into hot chocolate. Smells
sweet; tastes okay. For a while.

So pause with us and reflect. Prepare to consider with care
all of your investments within a comprehensive financial
plan. In essence, we need to review your investment of any
money into anything. Because whether you're buying a
DVD player, four years of private schooling for Marie, a cash-

mere sweater for Aunt Elizabeth, or stock shares of a fiber optics company, all these are investments coming out of your savings.

We're stating the intuitively obvious. Yet most weren't taught to treat each dip into the wallet as one in a series of investment decisions. Instead, with perhaps too little deliberation, we put an addition on the house. Or we borrowed at 8 percent to buy a Lexus. Or we splurged on a home entertainment center. There may be little wrong with this when we have the cash, but too many Americans don't. Too many spend money they don't have buying things they don't need, things which themselves depreciate rapidly.

Please reread that last sentence. It's at the heart of our financial troubles.

We'll step off the soapbox shortly, but the evidence here overwhelms us. Our personal savings rate as a nation has diminished over the past decade. The average adult has more than $5,000 of credit card debt at rates exceeding 17 percent per year. That's dangerous even in strong economic times. In a recession, that debt can level a family's finances.

The year 2001 brought recession, beginning in March. The results have included heavy job losses and salary cuts, making these times truly terrible for those riding large loans at high rates. Once you identify the difference between need and want, you begin to recognize a lot of this spending as overspending and misspending. The troubles they cause help us frame the questions we must answer in the coming pages. Namely:

1. What are the key automatic decisions we must make to spend our money more intelligently?
2. Should we refinance our mortgage?
3. What role do CDs play in money management?
4. How should we approach insurance?
5. What steps can we take to be ready for economic recovery, and to be better prepared the next (inevitable) time recession hits?

And many more questions besides. Let's answer them to-gether.

To get started, take these two steps:

## Step 1: Find Your Bearings

If you've been afraid to review your investment performance, now's the time. Your first task is to collect your most recent bro-kerage statements, your 401(k) and IRA accounts, and any other reports representing investments of your savings. Look at them, but don't dwell on them. In the pages ahead, we'll consider how you might change the allocation of these savings.

## Step 2: Rank Your Top Three Long-Term Financial Concerns, and Your Top Three Short-Term Financial Concerns

If you're having trouble sorting out your thoughts, start by list-ing every financial concern you have. Then place each item from your list into one of four groups, according to this anxi-ety scale:

1. "I don't know what to do. Every time I think about this, my heart races."
2. "This one makes my stomach roll, but I can repress it long enough to watch *Friends*."
3. "I'm occasionally plagued by a nagging voice reminding me that I should be doing more."
4. "I'm not that worried. I just need a little push."

With your concerns grouped by level of anxiety, you now have tasks at hand. The high-anxiety, high-priority items take first precedence. Then, you might as well get the high-anxiety, low-priority things out of the way as well. Our common goal is to eliminate high anxiety from your financial plans.

We asked our online community at Fool.com to share por-tions of their financial concerns lists. Take a look at what others worry about, marked with their anxiety rankings, and try to think about possible solutions to their (and your) concerns.

### Example No. 1: Married Fool with 1 Wife, 3 Children, 2 Dogs, and a House

Long-Term Concerns
- Funding college education for three kids. (1)
- Providing for family in the event of my untimely demise. (2)
- Retirement. (3)

Short-Term Concerns
- Being "smart" about my personal finances. For me, this means finding the best credit card and mortgage rates, sufficient savings and insurance, living below our means, etc. (2)
- Moving to be closer to work and to better schools. (3)
- My investment performance. (3)

### Example No. 2: Single, Renting Fool Who Likes to Shop

I'm twenty-five, single with no children, but two cats. I tackled a mountain of debt earlier in 2001 and have been saving ever since. Holding on to those savings, though, is not always easy. I like to shop for clothes and go out to eat—two high-cost habits I'll have a tough time abandoning.

Long-Term Concerns
- I've watched stocks plummet over the past year and have been burned on my choices. To boot, I'm not very interested in spending time on the subject, so I'm just holding on because I have no idea what to do next! (3)

Short-Term Concerns
- I'm not confident about my "emergency" savings stash. I feel like my long-term savings is on track, but I'm afraid that one trip to the mechanic will send me back into debt. (2)

- I plan to attend graduate school in a year or two, but I have no idea how to finance the education. If I can barely maintain my short-term savings, how am I going to finance an education and feed myself in the meantime? (4)

## Example No. 3: Married Fool in Transition
Short-Term Concerns

- I wish I had an emergency fund. I'm changing jobs and will have a month without any income (my new job starts in a few months). I sure wish I'd been one of those all-stars who keep three to six months of income set aside in an emergency fund. (2)
- My husband and I have implemented a loose budget. We watch groceries and spending money but assume that many line items are pretty fixed and not worth tracking. But there are still times each month when I don't have a good feel for how much cash we have. Sometimes we seem rich and sometimes broke. I wish I had a better sense of where the money goes. (4)

## Example No. 4: Married Fool, 1 Wife, 4 Children, and a New Job
Long-Term Concerns

- While we've saved a fair amount of money, we don't have anything specific set aside for the college education of our four kids (the oldest is almost twelve). (3)

Short-Term Concerns

- I recently changed jobs and have 401(k) accounts to roll over. (3)
- As a result of my recent job change, I was forced to liquidate a bunch of stock options, which I haven't yet reinvested in the market. I need to think about general asset allocation. I need, for example, to study the amount I'll invest in a new house in my new location. I have purposely been very conservative, given the economic and political volatility. (3)

# 6

# Timeless Suggestions for the Ideal You

> Whatever failures I have known, whatever errors I have committed, whatever follies I have witnessed in private and public life have been the consequence of action without thought.
>
> —BERNARD BARUCH

Having reflected and outlined your situation, you're starting the first chapter of this section already a hop, skip, and a jump toward improving your financial state. Let's now take another important step—ten of them, actually—by introducing the concept of the Ideal You. Specifically, we're going to ask ourselves what the Ideal You should look like—in all markets, in all economies. And then we're going to put on our blue suede shoes and take those important steps, one at a time, to help fashion the Ideal You.

## THE IDEAL YOU

Somewhere in our youth, we were given by our mother a small, thin, privately printed, orange-covered book with woodcut artwork entitled *The Magic Story*. We have just fetched the book off our shelf (yes, we keep our books for years and years). We see that it was written by Frederic Van Rensselaer Dey, whom we learn to be a popular dime novelist of a century ago (creator of detective Nick Carter), described in an appreciative introduction as "magnetic, brilliant, debonair, imperturbable, thirsty, unreliable and wholly charming . . . the typical handsome hero of the nineties." His forty-eight-page magic story goes thus:

A poor failure of an artist named Sturtevant wanders aimlessly through the streets of New York at the turn of the twentieth century. He hears of a magic story that seems to create success for all who encounter it. His curiosity as high as his spirits are low, Sturtevant stumbles into a bookstore and pays 3 cents for a ragged old scrapbook bound in rawhide. In it is the antiquated autobiography of an unknown author born in Virginia in 1642. The magic story.

In his twenties, its author had moved to Boston to work as a shipbuilding carpenter. Within five years, by 1670, he'd earned enough to buy the shipyard outright with men under his employ. Tragically, a fire spread through the yard. It burned his business to the ground. It ruined him financially, and drove him into debtors' prison. For a year, he sat in chains. And for years following his release, he wandered, despondent and weary. He did in the shadows of life.

Then, in a Poe-like waking slumber, in a roofless makeshift bed on a bitter cold night, the author encounters a warm, powerful, confident presence—a person who shockingly enough looks almost exactly like, but not quite, like him. He's discovered what he refers to as his double, a second self, his dual identity. He follows it for weeks before learning that it's his optimistic, enthusiastic self, his (Dey's words) "plus-entity." In effect, we have two complementary selves, the story suggests. Call it yin and yang, ego and id, Cheech and Chong, whatever you like. But what happens to us is that over the course of our lives one of these identities begins to take hold. For better or worse.

In the narrator's own case, he has allowed his "minus-entity" to drive out his better half so completely that the better half (the Cheech, if you will) had actually left his body altogether. His simple realization is that his Other Self, his positive identity, exists. It's just an arm's-length away. And bringing that side back into consciousness is what will lead him (and his readers) to success, prosperity, "magic."

The storyteller draws what we consider to be two wonderful lessons, applicable to your life, your profession, and your financial plan:

1. Failure exists only in the grave.
2. Whatsoever you desire of good is yours. You have but to stretch forth your hand and take it.

We won't spend any more paper on "plus-entities" and "minus-entities," but we will return to the twenty-first century and admit that we have—perhaps each of us has—this Ideal Me in mind who is perfectly organized, Swiss-watch-exact, Thoreau-efficient. The Ideal Me makes every financial decision flawlessly. The Ideal Me never gets parking tickets. The Ideal Me is helpful, purposeful, prosperous. The Ideal Me is an incorrigible enthusiast for life, always prepared ahead of time for any eventuality. Most of us probably never come close to approaching this person. (We both insist the other doesn't.) However, the Ideal Me does give us something to shoot for, which is generally the purpose of ideals, and of magic, no?

And shoot we will.

## WHAT'S IT TAKE TO BE IDEAL?

Believe it or not, out of the hundreds of financial tasks out there, you're a mere ten steps away from getting a lot closer to the Ideal Financial You. Over the next eighteen pages, we'll outline each of these steps, intent upon helping you complete them. Then, at the end of this chapter, we present the "10 Steps to the Ideal You Tally Sheet," where you can check 'em off as you complete 'em.

One helpful starting point is that our suggested acts are ordered by general priority. The items at the top of the list, in our estimation, are more important than the ones that follow. However, you should also refer back to your personal priority list to match your anxieties to our suggestions. As you work through the list, you should notice that certain steps fit pretty well together. For example, you might want to tackle all of the insurance steps together to save you time.

Each step contains a plan and one or more actions you can take. In many cases, you can accomplish these on your own, particularly if you're a highly motivated do-it-yourselfer. But with each we've also included additional ideas or pointers to resources to help you further, where needed.

Okay, let's begin.

## Step 1: The Financial Plan

"The Plan" is just a list of your goals, an estimate of how much they cost, and a reckoning of how you're going to pay for them. At its core, your financial plan should tell you what you have and what kinds of investments and returns you'll need to achieve your goals. We believe that everyone in America should have a plan. If you don't have one, your chances are so much smaller of getting from here to there. Below we'll help you begin to make a plan, but please know also that it can be quite a deep process, sometimes demanding personalization that could be outside the scope of this book or any other. If you wish it, we have an outstanding fee-only service called TMF Money Advisor that, for a fraction of what you'd pay a financial planner, helps you work up your own plan with the help of Motley Fool seminars, an online interactive planning tool, and exclusive phone access to ask any question under the sun of your own objective counselor. The key to this Motley Fool service is that it is salesman-free—the advice you'll get is completely independent and therefore totally focused on your best interests. In a world full of people who are going to charge you money up front and then hope to get you with annual fees on the back end, this is rare. If you're interested in taking TMF Money Advisor for a free trial, visit TMFMA.Fool.com for more information.

Okay, let's set to. Depending on the level of detail you want, your plan could take you anywhere from one hour to forever (if you get obsessed!). Here's what it takes to check "Financial Plan" off your tally sheet:

1. Write down your goals.
List your financial goals in any order. These should include everything from buying a new high-definition TV to sending the kids to college to going on annual vacations to retiring to buying a house to paying off your debt. Anything that you think will cost you more than $250 should be included in your plan.

2. Find out what they're going to cost.
You better believe it: Find out what they're gonna cost! Some of them you know already, others you can estimate— do some homework, ask a friend. For estimating your bigger investments, we do have some online calculators for those who are Internet-inclined. They'll help you plan financially for everything from buying a house, buying a car, paying for college, and raising children, to managing your debt and funding your retirement plans. These calculators can serve as the workshop tools of your complete financial plan. Here's the Web address, if you're interested: Fool.com/calcs/calculators.htm.

You have now priced out your spending, having ranked your needs.

3. Match what you already have to where you're going.
The next step is to value your present assets; we need to detail what you have now. The point isn't to spend hours totting up everything you call yours. You just want an approximate figure. To begin, consider dividing up your assets into three broad categories:

- *Cash:* checking and savings accounts, cash in broker-age accounts, money markets, and CDs.

- *Long-term savings:* IRA and 401(k) balances, stocks, bonds, mutual funds, exercised stock options, cash value of life insurance.

- *Fixed assets:* housing, jewelry, cars, art, and anything else meaningful that can be sold on eBay.

With a good read on your present assets, and from Step 2 a good read on your desired future assets, you now know the difference between the two. Congratulations. You're among a tiny minority of Americans who have actually thought about this and now tried to put numbers to it.

That gap between what you have now and what you hope to have will have to be bridged. How do you do it? A combination of savings and investment, obviously. The investment part we'll talk about later. Let's talk about savings.

4. Yes, it's time to budget.

You don't necessarily need a budget to generate savings and complete your plan. But why not? It needn't take much time and can identify opportunities for greater savings. As a guideline, we offer the following three approaches:

- *The whole-baked budget:* This one demands tracking every expense for the year, keeping receipts, and then seeing where you could cut back in order to fund your goals. Quicken or Microsoft Money software are highly recommended.

- *The half-baked budget:* This one requires only that you boil down your spending into broad categories. Simply choose the two or three biggest expense categories—such as food, entertainment, and shopping. Track only these primary categories, breaking them down into subgroups to your heart's delight.

- *The un-baked budget:* Ahh, so you want to do even less than these? We sympathize. The Un-Baked Budget can work wonders. Just track your results for a single month. Put your income on one side, then all your expenses on the other. Add up all of your must-pay monthly bills (housing, groceries, utilities, transportation costs, insurance, credit card minimums, etc.), then subtract the total from your income. Next, pull out your allotment of savings. You'll be left with your discretionary income. Getting just this far in the budgeting process will at least shine a little bit of light on your financial life, a light of coming prosperity.

5. An easy alternative solution.
If you found yourself blenching at Steps 1–4, let's just remind you again that first of all, this is important. Again, everyone in America who harbors any hope to retire in comfort should be operating off their own financial plan. Second, you don't have to do it all yourself. If you really don't want to do any of this at all, find a fee-only financial planner and convince your spouse to meet with 'em. If on the other hand you do want to make an effort but are feeling a bit overwhelmed by the hands-on nature of Steps 1–4, we'll remind you again of our TMF Money Advisor service. Whether you use our service or someone else's, and to whatever extent you involve yourself personally in the process, please work to check Step 1 off your tally sheet at the end of the chapter. We've listed the steps by priority, and this was the first.

## Step 2: Getting Rid of That Debt

With a basic plan in place, if you're like us you're eyeing your debts critically. The more money that goes to paying interest on your principal debt, the less you have for your future goals and for life. On top of that, your credit rating can affect every aspect of your financial life, from what you can buy, to how much a loan costs, even to where you can live.

If you have no meaningful debt, great. Flip right to the tally sheet at the end of this chapter and check this one off. But if you do, today is the day to begin getting out of it.

Here are the key points, in order:

1. Figure out where you stand.
If you're starting from scratch, separate out the "good debt" (student loans, mortgage, and investments in things that might grow in value) from the bad debt (credit cards, store charge cards, car loans).

2. Plan your payoff order.
Aim to pay off your debts in order from highest interest rates to lowest. That's right, we said highest interest rates to lowest—not highest amounts to lowest. We receive calls to our radio show all the time from people who think they should be paying off their biggest balance. Nay, dear reader. Think of the interest rates you're being charged as "penalties." You want to get rid of your biggest penalties first.

3. Pick up the phone.
As we have written in our starter money book *You Have More than You Think* (which contains more depth on eliminating credit card debt, if that's what you're looking for), you can negotiate down the interest rates on your cards one by one, and you should! Credit card companies compete for your business all the time—use that. Shop around to other lenders online or off-, and locate some lower rates. Then let your existing creditor know that you're going to move your business to the new firm that is offering the more attractive rate. If it doesn't work, move your business.

4. Head back to that budget.
Go back to your budget and make sure you account for your debt payments in there. You need to be paying off more than the minimums. A $1,000 debt on a credit card carrying an in-

terest rate of 18 percent will take nineteen years to pay off if you only make the minimum payments. Gasp!

5. Make regular check-ups.
Not obtaining a copy of your credit report is like avoiding the dentist; it'll come back to haunt you. It's also the first step to guaranteeing a long happy credit history. Order up your credit report. If you're looking for a quick, safe, and reputable way to do it online, just point your Internet browser to Fool.com/credit and review Step 10: The Credit Report.

There, you can order your credit report and obtain some of our other tips for getting out of high-interest-rate debt.

6. Make sure your credit report is error-free and start polishing it.
Errors turn up all the time in the world of credit, so make sure there are none on your report. If there are errors, you'll need to mail in information to bring your report up to date. Do so. And if your record is less than squeaky clean, there are three things that will improve a bad credit report: time, your discipline, and reestablished credit.

The Motley Fool is serious about helping you get out of debt; it is one of our primary focuses. At Fool.com, we've taken great pleasure in watching some of our customers pay off as much as $75,000 in high-interest debt through inspired discipline, and with the help of our community. If you wish to join in, make sure you stop by one of our most popular community haunts, the Consumer Credit discussion board. You can locate the board by visiting boards.Fool.com, then type in credit cards in the search box.

## Step 3: Pad Yourself with Cash
Now, it's on to your savings. Let's start with the short-term loot, which is your number-one defense against debt.

Having money on hand for that valve job, honeymoon, or unemployment notice will help keep you off the credit card and out of your long-term savings.

We want you to know we draw a distinction between the pile of savings for the family vacation and your three-month cash cushion. Make no mistake about it, your three-month (or six-month) cushion should be your rainy-day fund. It's the money you can fall back on when unexpected or not so unexpected emergencies hit. It should not be touched except in case of emergency.

The most important step is to accumulate your cash cushion. But there's a second often overlooked step—finding the right place to keep that money. Here's how to put it all together.

1. Figure out how much you need.
Figure out how much you spend each month on necessities like food, shelter, transportation to work, and anything that you've promised your kids. Bump up this number a tad so you can afford things like job-hunting expenses should you suddenly find yourself out looking. Then multiply the number by three or six, depending on how many months you suspect you'll need. If you're a single free-spirited daredevil, go with three. If you're a primary caregiving planner, go with six.

2. Figure out how much you can contribute and just do it.
Make sure that this fits into your budget. Make it one of your must-pay expenses. If you're having trouble saving, we highly recommend an automatic transfer program.

3. Pick the right kind of account.
Since we're talking about your emergency savings here, put the cash somewhere you'll be able to get your hands on it . . . in case of an emergency. That narrows it down to:

- High-yield savings accounts
- Money market accounts
- Money market funds

4. Start comparison shopping.

Look at bank ads in newspapers, check out bankrate.com, and see what brokers are offering on cash accounts. As you shop, think about the following questions:

- What interest rate does it pay?
- How risk-tolerant are you?
- What will it cost to purchase and maintain the investment?

And if you're looking for high returns, but don't feel like you have the time to do the research, consider yourself lucky to be a Fool. MBNA offers special yields for Motley Fools. Visit savings.Fool.com.

## 🃏 Step 4: Life Insurance

Life insurance only matters if you have dependents. If you're single and have no one else relying on your income, you can pass it over (that'll make some insurance salesmen choke . . . but it's true). Of course, flag this page if you're planning for offspring someday.

Insurance, especially life insurance, can be a real buzz kill. Why? It's confusing, it's administrative, and we're talking about the end of your life here. That said, it provides for kids, a spouse, an elderly parent—everyone that counts on you for a paycheck. A good life insurance package replaces your income when you die (perish the thought).

If you already have life insurance, you probably want to make sure you have the right coverage. If you don't, let's get it done. Here are a few key steps to getting it right.

1. Consider a convertible term policy for your life insurance needs.

For starters, most people are better off with straightforward term insurance. It's simpler, more flexible, and easier to price-shop. (Insert choking sounds from salesmen again.

Few sales commissions may be had in the world of inexpensive, effective term insurance.) You should look for the least expensive option that meets your needs, but make sure that it's guaranteed renewable without a medical exam. We also suggest a convertible term policy, which will give you the option of converting to a cash value policy—a potentially useful option with negligible extra cost.

2. Determine how much you'll need.
The rule of thumb is that life insurance should replace 80 percent of your pretax income. Don't overlook stay-at-home moms and dads either; it will cost you plenty to replace their child care and other indispensable contributions.

3. Buy the insurance.
One of the great things about term life insurance is that it's very easy to compare prices. Look for two things: a) price and b) the company's financial health. Financial health is measured by the letter grades A++ (very good) to F (very bad). Look for the best prices at the A+ and higher firms. If you want our help checking into life insurance, visit us online at insurance.Fool.com.


## Step 5: Make a Will

Hey, it's time to meet with an attorney! Come on, get excited with us.

Okay, so you're not looking forward to venturing into the world of file cabinets, leather-bound copies of Grisham books, incessant wordplay, and high hourly fees. Understood. But you need a will. You really do. Because you will die. And it won't take long or cost much (the will, at least).

If you don't write a will and you have any meaningful assets, well, you just fouled up things for your dependents. Your will details exactly what happens to your property (and potentially your children—er, "minor dependents") when you die. You'll definitely want a lawyer for this one. If you want to do it on your own, you can opt for preprinted, fill-in-the-blanks forms and software. Just be sure they're up to date and conform to the laws of your state.

So, thy will be done. Shall we?

1. If you don't already have an attorney, you want one that specializes in estate planning.

- First, if you're already using a fine lawyer in a specific area (such as an income tax advisor), ask for a referral. The pros work together, know each other in many cases, and have opinions of one another.

- If you're a babe in the woods without experts on your current personal staff, don't go to the Yellow Pages just yet. Instead, speak with family, friends, and business associates. Encourage them to praise or trash their current counsel. Then follow up with the best of 'em.

- If those resources aren't available to you, contact the local chapter or national office of the American Bar Association to find someone who specializes in estate planning in your area.

2. Prepare for your meeting.
Have a clear understanding of what you own and where you want those assets to go should you die. Know how those assets are presently titled. Title may negate any provision in a will. The same is true if assets like retirement accounts and your life insurance package name beneficiaries. If you have minors, know who you want as a guardian in the event both parents are deceased.

3. Get two checks for the price of one.
While you're there, take care of your durable power of attorney and medical power of attorney (that's Step 10, right around the corner).

## Step 6: Disability Insurance

Ahh, more insurance. But we have to take care of the basics here. Disability insurance is like life insurance in that it protects your future income. With disability insurance, though, the income protection comes in case of an inability to work because of poor health or injury.

Coming after a death-driven step, we can also likewise assert that no one likes to imagine getting hurt, or so sick that they can't work. But these things happen out there every day—and sometimes "out there" can be "right here." Degenerative disabling diseases and accidents are sad realities of the human condition. It's best to prepare for the worst while hoping for the best.

Everyone who works needs disability insurance!

Everyone.

Even people with no dependents and high salaries and large cash savings need to make sure they have disability insurance. Life insurance protects your income for those around you in case of your death. But disability insurance protects you, plus any dependents, if you find yourself unable to work. Even single folks with no kids need their income protected.

Some employers provide disability insurance, but you need to check on exactly what you're getting. Ask questions about it at work. And if you're self-employed or your employer doesn't offer disability, you can shop for a single plan. However, be forewarned that you'll pay more for private disability insurance than for life insurance. We've compiled a list of disability providers to give you a push in the right direction in our Insurance Center at insurance.Fool.com.

Unfortunately disability insurance is one of the toughest insurance products to buy online, and tough too via quick phone calls to direct insurance providers. So here's the skinny on this one:

Make sure your policy includes these must-haves. Whether you have disability insurance or not, you need to shop around for insurance to make sure your policy includes these:

Must-have:

- Percent of income replaced: between 60 percent and 80 percent.
- Long-term disability covered to sixty-five years of age (not just five or ten years).
- Liberal definition of disability, including mental illness, stress disorders, back pain, and severe migraines, just to name a few common maladies that keep people out of the workforce.

Could be important:

- Does the plan define commissions, bonuses, and over-time as income to be replaced? If a significant portion of your income comes from these sources, you should be sure they're covered.
- What's the maximum monthly payment? (High-wage employees may get cut off at a certain level.)

## Step 7: Open a Roth IRA

An Individual Retirement Arrangement (IRA), more commonly referred to as individual retirement account, is a retirement savings plan available to anyone who receives taxable compensation during the year. And a Roth IRA offers you huge tax breaks on your retirement savings when you withdraw the funds after the age of fifty-nine and a half. You have to pay taxes on the money you put into a Roth IRA account, but that money then grows tax-free (excepting any early withdrawals).

Besides your budget, most components of the Ideal You ensure that you've built a safety net. (The Ideal You is financially bulletproof!) This step, on the other hand, encourages you to look toward the future and sock away moolah for the golden years. So, why a Roth IRA? Consider these benefits:

- Tax-free growth: While you won't get a tax deduction on contributions to a Roth IRA, you'll never have to pay taxes on the earnings when you begin withdrawals (assuming you follow the rules).

- More control: If you open your account with a discount broker, you can purchase individual stocks, bonds, and any index investment offered through that broker. This is an advantage over the limited selection offered by most employer-sponsored plans.

- No mandatory distributions: With employer-sponsored plans and traditional IRAs, you must begin withdrawing funds by (this is a bit of a tongue twister) "April of the year following the year in which you reach age 70½, even if you don't need the money." Okay, our heads are still spinning. But none of those guidelines apply to a Roth account. If you don't need the money, it can keep growing on its merry, tax-free way.

Your ability to contribute to a Roth begins to phase out at a modified adjusted gross income of $95,000 for single filers and $150,000 for joint filers, reaching the ineligible stage at $110,000 and $160,000, respectively.

How much you can contribute: Thanks to the recent tax cut, it's a good time to be saving for retirement. The contribution limit for a Roth (and traditional IRA as well)—here come lotsa numbers—increased to $3,000 for 2002 through 2004; $4,000 for 2005 through 2007; and $5,000 for 2008. Thereafter, the $5,000 maximum allowable contribution will be indexed to inflation in $500 increments.

Here are your key steps to starting your Roth IRA account:

1. Find a place to invest your cash.
A discount brokerage account is a logical place to house your long-term retirement savings. Maybe you already have one. And maybe you're even happy with the brokerage firm. If not, visit our IRA Center at The Motley Fool to compare each of our sponsoring brokers' IRA offerings and fees: ira.Fool.com.

Two particular things to note as you shop:

- Fees. By law, your broker can charge an annual fee to maintain your IRA, but many don't.
- Trading commissions. Make sure the bulk of your contribution is going toward your retirement nest egg, not to trading commissions.

2. Open an account.

Setting up an IRA account is usually as easy as downloading the application forms, signing them, and folding them nicely into an envelope with a check to fund your account. You'll receive confirmation of your ability to invest.

3. Invest.

Consider your IRA account the basket that holds your retirement money. You get to decide what goes in that basket. That means deciding which stocks or mutual funds you want to buy. (Hint: If you're new at this or just don't have the time to evaluate individual stocks, consider an index fund to get started. It may be all you need. More on that to come.)

## Step 8: Liability Insurance

Drats! More insurance! But this one is also critical.

If you're found legally responsible for injuries or property damage suffered by others, liability insurance will pay the bill, up to the limit of your coverage. It also provides a legal defense should your insurance company decide to argue your liability in court. Such liability coverage usually comes with car, home, or renter's insurance.

In all likelihood, you probably have some liability insurance. If you don't or don't know, let's make that step one. Step two is figuring out if you really have enough. Here's how to get it done:

1. If you don't have any liability coverage . . .

- Get homeowner's or renter's insurance. For the money, the liability insurance that comes with these policies is a powerful defense. It not only protects you around your home but, in general, also covers you and your dependents outside the home. A good place to start looking for insurance quotes is the Insweb homeowner's/renter's coverage section available at insweb.com.

- If you have a car and don't have insurance, nice try! Buy some immediately. Every state requires it by law. And buckle up, dear Fool!

2. Making sure you have enough . . .

- Figure out what you already have. For your home-owner's or renter's policy, you want personal liability coverage. For your automobile insurance, there are two basic types of liability coverage: bodily injury covers "people costs" (the injured party's medical bills, lost wages, pain and suffering), while property damage covers the injured party's damaged property.

- Look carefully at your automobile insurance liability limits. Each state enforces its own minimum limits, but don't count on these to give you sufficient coverage. Their coverage is pretty meager. Also, don't be fooled by your state's "no fault" law. These laws don't exempt you from big-dollar lawsuits. They just make it tougher for others to sue for routine, small-potatoes damages.

- Determine if you need more. This is one of the few areas of insurance that unfortunately don't have a handy rule of thumb to hang our caps on. Ultimately it's a subjective decision, but we'll at least try to set the stage for you:

A common insurance industry recommendation is to maximize both your auto's and homeowner's/renter's policies' liability limits (usually $300,000 is the ceiling for each) and then tack on what's called an umbrella or excess coverage policy up to $1 million. It's usually cheapest to do the whole deal (auto, homeowner's/renter's, and umbrella) through one insurance company.

Whether this boilerplate advice makes sense for you depends mostly upon your odds of being sued. There are some characteristics that greatly increase your odds of being sued—like owning a business, your lifestyle, the lifestyle of your dependents, and your personal wealth and fame.

Beyond a $1 million umbrella policy, the question becomes even more subjective. Although judgments in the tens of millions of dollars are remotely possible, covering all such possibilities is prohibitively expensive. Basically, you have to do the cost versus risk calculation in your gut and pick an upper limit that makes sense to you.

- Get more coverage if you need it. If you're looking to add auto, homeowner's/renter's, or umbrella coverage, remember to check with your existing insurance company first. It's usually cheapest to do through one insurance company.

## Step 9: Living Will

Also called an advance medical directive, a living will is a document that asserts you want the right to die a natural death, free of all costly, extraordinary efforts to maintain your life when that life can only be sustained by artificial means.
It makes the decision easier on the doctor, the hospital, and

your family. Used in conjunction with a medical power of attorney, this tool can spare your family a painful, drawn-out, and costly process.

Play ball:

1. Get a copy of the form at any local hospital or you can download one from the following site: nwjustice.org/docs/9501.html.

2. Complete the form and make a copy. Then tell your loved ones about the living will and let them know where they can find it. 'Nuff said.

## Step 10: Durable Power of Attorney AND Medical Power of Attorney

Okay, we've reached Step 10. Cleansing breath, cleansing breath, cleansing breath. Ahhhhhhhhhh.

If you have accomplished any single one of the steps above, you have taken one strong step toward a better financial situation that you and your loved ones will appreciate. Give yourself a pat on the back—or better yet, get them to give you a pat on the back because, well, they should! It's about the least they could do. Listen, we know this stuff isn't the easiest or most pleasurable way to spend your time. However, putting into action many of the steps above may in time prove to have been among the best decisions you've ever made. Further, a bunch of them are one-timers.

If you have accomplished more than just one of those above—if you have accomplished some or even all of them—you may well have gotten done more than your authors have. Listen, we're not perfect, either. The point is this is the Ideal You, and the Ideal Us. Anyway, this checklist is one you can return to in time, because in its own way it's timeless, as relevant in good times as in bad. These are the things the Ideal You will have accomplished. We're not satisfied to think we just helped you make the team—we're working on churning out Personal Finance League All-Stars!

So now, Step 10, the powers of attorney docs. These documents allow you to select a person to make decisions on your behalf—financial and legal in the first case, medical in the second case—when you're incapacitated.

Again, this is more a "when" and less an "if." Insurance company statisticians (a colorful bunch, no doubt) tell us that prior to age fifty we have a one-in-three chance of being disabled for longer than ninety days. That disability may mean we become physically or mentally incapable of acting for ourselves. Both of these documents allow the person you select to make decisions on your behalf. Without those documents, your family will be forced to hire an attorney, go to court, and have someone appointed as your conservator and/or guardian to make decisions and conduct business on your behalf. That's a serious pain. It's needless, time-consuming, and costly. Particularly since it can be avoided with one or two inexpensive documents that an attorney can prepare today.

Here's how to take that final step toward becoming the Ideal You:

1. Pick someone whom you trust to be your power of attorney and discuss it with them. Make sure that the person you pick will be comfortable making decisions and is willing to accept the responsibility.

2. Visit an attorney to execute the papers.


## CHAPTER CONCLUSION: WHERE IS THE IDEAL YOU?

Again, don't worry if the magical "plus-entity" Ideal You isn't yet ideally realized.

(By the way, while it has its useful point, you don't think we're taking this whole magical "plus-entity" stuff at serious face value, do you?—c'mon now, you need to get to know us better—we're having a bit of fun out here.)

To reiterate, we only checked about half of these items. No surprise: We're not yet ideal, either. However, our Motley Fool checklist lights a clear path of direction. It lets you know what you haven't done, and the general order in which it should be tackled. And if you are looking for any inspiration here, any extra push at all, you've come to the right page. Because here is a wonderful note sent to us by a Fool in our online community who knows the importance of completing these ten steps. After reading them, he wrote to us (please note that the asides in parentheses are his own):

> Can anyone be genuinely thankful for personal finance? I am.
>
> A couple of years ago I was at the top of my game professionally. I had finally hit the big leagues (for me) in salary and stock options. Not being extravagant by nature, we had the luxury of having pretty much everything we wanted: living where we wanted, going where we wanted, doing what we wanted. In nearly every way that mattered to us, we had it made.
>
> I did have a nuisance pain that was inconvenient and decided to have some outpatient surgery to correct it. The surgery was on a Thursday, then I'd be back in the office on Monday. I'd be back even before my voice mail could fill up. Unfortunately, I didn't recover as quickly as expected. One night I woke up screaming in pain. By the time I arrived at the emergency room, I felt like I was dying. Turns out I was having one of those very rare complications anyone can get from surgery and it was, in fact, nearly killing me.
>
> I spent four days in critical care and another couple in the noncritical ward. I knew I was in trouble the first time I opened my eyes. What did I see? Friends and family around my bed who had flown in that day. I'd watched enough TV to know that same-day travel meant they thought there was a pretty good chance I would die. Happily, I didn't.
>
> So what does this have to do with being thankful for personal finance?

Well, those six days in the hospital—just the hospital—ended up costing more than $32,000. And we continued to get bills from doctors and tests from the hospital stay for literally another year, with the final tally up over $35,000. (How's your medical insurance?) My recovery was slow and painful, and I wasn't consistently working for six months. (How's your disability insurance?) During most of the first year after surgery, I had daily medication, weekly tests, and numerous complications requiring appointments with equally numerous specialists. (How's that medical insurance holding up?)

I now had hard proof that life was unsafe: Random stuff could jump up out of nowhere and try to kill you. On top of all the physical problems, I was now paralyzed by fear as well. So off I went to therapy to combat the fear. (Still with me on the medical insurance or are you spending cash now?)

An extraordinary burden fell on my spouse throughout my recovery. My spouse was with me 24/7 in the hospital. Luckily we had friends who cared for the house and the animals while we were at the hospital. (If you don't have friends or family, you're going to be paying money for these services—how are your cash reserves?) All of my spouse's existing vacation time from work was used up while I was in the hospital, but once I went home I needed her with me so she took another two weeks off work without pay. (Are your cash reserves hanging in there?)

Trying to work, care for me, and keep the house running was grinding my spouse down to a nub. After two months we decided my spouse would quit working until we could figure out which end was up with me. (Is your lifestyle lagging your finances so you have some wiggle room?)

My employer was very understanding and accommodating during my recovery. Unfortunately, my body had thirty hours/week of stamina in it, yet my job had seventy hours/week of responsibility. With a lot of help from a lot of people, we made it work. My spouse continued not to work because I was still worthless around the house. I gave whatever I had to work, came home, and collapsed. After several months, it became clear that my body wasn't getting what it needed to recover fully and my work responsibilities weren't getting what they needed to thrive. So we had to look at options.

Early retirement had always been a priority for us and we were allocating our money appropriately. (Are you consistently and proactively investing in the things that are most important to you?) But we had no intention of retiring until our forties. In fact, we weren't paying much attention at all to the performance of our retirement investments. (Are you regularly monitoring your investments and tracking their actual performance against your expected performance?)

At first, we couldn't tell if we had enough money invested to retire because we had never run the numbers or done the research. (Do you know what your magic numbers are for your most important financial goals?) Once we ran the numbers, we were happy to find out we could retire. So we walked away from the salary and the stock options, admittedly with numerous people questioning our sanity, and retired early.

Now, I didn't have a will/trust in place when I had my surgery. I'd always assumed that everything of value had a beneficiary statement and I was too young for anything serious to happen. Once I got back on my feet, we went directly to a good estate lawyer. Found out a few interesting things. While everything of value did, in fact, have designated beneficiaries, not all of the documents had been updated appropriately when I submitted changes many years earlier. If I had died, my spouse would've had some nasty financial surprises. (When was the last time you double-checked your beneficiary statements?) And other investments were held in such a way as to leave my spouse with seriously adverse tax consequences. (Are you getting the consultation/advice of professionals when you're making major financial decisions?)

Admittedly, what happened to me was extraordinary. I never imagined I would have a life-threatening medical problem in my thirties.

My point is that stuff happens. Hopefully it will never happen to you, but it can and it might. Do the things you can do now so you don't add

financial worries on top of everything else. We were dumb lucky—I hope
you're smarter than we were and rely on more than dumb luck for
yourself. Set up your finances so that you can handle an emergency.
Make sure you're adequately and appropriately insured. Meet with a
good lawyer to ensure that your estate is set up the way you want it
to be. That way, if stuff ever happens to you, at the very least you and
the people you love can be thankful for personal finance too.

Dear Fool, please remember that the things on our list are
the true bricks and mortar of your financial foundation. They
may or may not match with your top priorities or anxieties
from the previous chapter. Yet if you look closely, you should
start to see how the two lists are really intertwined. As someone approaching the Ideal You, you'll be better poised to
tackle some of your larger savings goals and focus on maximizing these returns.

We needn't prolong things further. This book will repay
you its cost many times over if you simply accomplish any
one of this chapter's checklist items, let alone several. Each
involves thousands of dollars' worth of meaning for you
and your loved ones, and takes you one step closer to the
Ideal You.

And that's the true magic of this story.

## 10 STEPS TO THE IDEAL YOU
## TALLY SHEET

Here it is, the all-in-one, do-it-yourself perfection kit! All you
have to do is check off those things that you've completed or
set a personal due date for yourself to complete a task. It is
our opinion that, depending on your financial and physical
condition, a concerted effort on your part could result in the
completion of all ten items in a single day.

Handy directions: Photocopy this checklist and keep it either on your refrigerator or as the cover sheet to those metic-
ulously filed financial documents.

_____        1. Complete or reprioritize your financial
                          plan.
_____           Write down goals
_____           List and rank costs
_____           Create a budget
_____           Review plan once a year

_____        2. Get out of debt.
_____           Set a target date
_____           Plan your payoff order
_____           Check your credit history

_____        3. Create a three- to six-month cash
                          cushion.
_____           Set your plan
_____           Start saving
_____           Open the right account

_____        4. Get life insurance or double-check your
                          coverage.
_____           Calculate the policy amount
_____           Buy that insurance

_____        5. Make a will.
_____           Find an attorney
_____           Prepare for your appointment

_____        6. Get disability insurance.
_____           Check your policy against the must-have list
_____           Get with your employer first

_____        7. Open a Roth IRA.
_____           Open an account
_____           Max out your contributions

_____    8. Get liability insurance or make sure you
have enough coverage.

_____    Review your existing policies

_____    Get more coverage, as needed

_____    9. Execute a living will.

_____    Talk over the decision with your family

_____    10. Sign a durable power of attorney and
medical power of attorney.

_____    Talk over the decision with your family

_____    See an attorney to complete it

# 7

# Timely Suggestions for the Particular You

They that will not be counseled, cannot be helped. If you do
not hear reason, she will rap you on the knuckles.

—BENJAMIN FRANKLIN

Okay, if you are not yet on the way toward being a more
Ideal You, we have at least lit your path. And the path we've
sent you down is very much a timeless Everyman journey. The
actions to take are ones that you would want to take regardless of the age or year or season, or direction the wind happens to be blowing.

Timeless perspective on your finances counts for a lot. But
timely perspective is equally valuable. And together, we all
happen to be living through:

- A very poor eighteen months of stock market performance
- A world that doesn't feel as safe or predictable as it
  once did
- A weak economy with a record number of layoffs

What can and should you be doing right now in addition to
your ten tasks? Well, there's an old tale about a fox chasing a

rabbit down a straightaway. Surprisingly, the rabbit outruns and eludes him. "How could a rabbit possibly outrun a fox?" is the question. The answer is simple. The fox was running for its supper; the rabbit was running for its life.

What's this have to do with your finances? One of our biggest challenges together is to feel more of that rabbitlike sense of urgency—that sense of something important being at stake (our financial future). We must take our finances seriously now. So our short list of new "foxes" above can and should be a motivating, not enervating, set of circumstances, which we can use to get done what we need to get done now—to get a financial plan in place.

Good news: While being the *timeless* Ideal You will put a good bit of distance between you and the foxes, the world *in the very short term* is actually providing some time-specific opportunities helping you profit. Even if you feel you've recently lost lots of financial ground, we challenge you to tweak your thinking.

Here then is a secondary list of five timely actions to consider in the face of the here and now:

## 1. Reprioritize Your Budget

Business as usual is no longer business as usual. Many people have been forced out of jobs, while others have watched their savings get cut in half over the past two years. We simply have to keep better track, therefore, of the dollars we have. If you don't have a budget, that will mean doing your first-ever budget (Step 1 on your tally sheet). If you do have a budget, but constructed it a while ago—or if it is in any way a little flabby or out of touch—it's time in this recessionary environment to consider rebudgeting.

- Building your budget from scratch. Must this be onerous? No. Remember that we gave you three approaches to getting that budget done. Getting a handle on where the heck your money goes is, for many Americans, the single most powerful financial activity. Knowledge is

power, and if you lack the knowledge of how much
you're spending and where it's being spent, those foxes'll
always outrun you.

- Make a game of it, if you need to. Try to underspend in
  the second week what you spent in the first. Then take
  half that difference and buy your significant other a small
  inspirational gift as a token of your new commitment to
  living below your means.

- Finally, rebudget once every year, once every six months
  if you're feeling ambitious.

## 2. Refinance Everything

We were tempted initially just to write, "Refinance your
home." On its own, that'd be a very good thing. Refinancing
a mortgage at these lower interest rates is as close to an automatically good blanket decision as we ever get. Lower rates
generally mean lower payments, which is why you should refinance in conjunction with Step 1 above. Your new budget
should reflect this beneficial new reality.

However, this can go deeper. You may be able to lower
other payments, interest and otherwise, in this economy.
We're all having a heck of a time, which is why you'll get a
knowing nod when you explain to your financier or your
landlord that you're going to need to lower your payments in
this environment, or risk moving your business or (worst of
all) defaulting. We said a "knowing nod," but whether that's a
"sympathetic nod" or not, we cannot say for sure. But the
worst they can do is say no, right?

Interest rates are incredibly low. The fed funds rate continues below 2 percent and if Greenspan whacks much more at
rates, they'll go negative! Well, okay, not negative. But interest
rates are at their lowest in forty years. You should be paying
low rates on any money you borrow. For example, credit card
interest rates on your balances, there's another great thing to

refinance. Get them below 10 percent, then pay it all down, posthaste.

Refinance everything.

## 3. Take Losses and Reduce Capital Gains

Despite an extremely poor two-year stock market (the only real "millennium bug" that ever showed up), many investors continue to ride significant capital gains from the preceding five years. And yet, if you're like us, you've initiated some new positions over the past twenty-four months that are way underwater. (We understand that if you go deep enough in the ocean, the water actually clocks in below the freezing point—that's how far down a few of our stocks are.)

That's why this is actually an outstanding time to cash out of your losers and generate substantial capital losses that may be used to offset existing capital gains. Before the year is out, take a hard look at any portfolios you're privileged enough to manage, and consider ditching all positions that are in the red. After a two-year stock market like we've had, many of us could or should be able to reduce capital gains taxes to zilch, through prudent maneuvering.

It should go without saying . . . but . . . obviously, for investments in a tax-advantaged environment—such as an IRA, 401(k), SEP-IRA, 403(b), etc.—you'll realize no tax consequences if you decide to sell certain stocks, regardless of whether you sell at a profit or loss. But for investments that are not in a tax-deferred account, your decision of what and when to sell could be critical for your taxes. So listen up—here's what you need to know:

1. Sell the right shares (see below).
2. Be careful when dumping stocks you might want to rebuy.
3. Think about using the "super-long-term gain" and "deemed sale" election to your advantage (ask about these via TMF Money Advisor, or see a tax professional as needed).
4. Get rid of your worthless stock.

Nota bene: There are right and wrong shares to sell.

Not all shares of stock are created equal. Here's a quick example:

On January 10, you purchase 1,000 shares of Wizzbang Incorporated for $15 a share. The stock does well, so on February 25 you purchase another 1,000 shares for $35 a share. Wizzbang Inc. has some problems, and the stock slips back to $32 a share. You tell your broker to sell 1,000 shares on April 12. Your broker deposits $32,000 into your account (let's ignore brokerage commissions for the purpose of our discussion).

Life is good . . . or is it?

Well, which shares did you sell? On first blush, you might not think it matters. But look closer and you'll see that it matters a great deal. If you sold the first block of shares (the January 10 shares), you'll recognize a taxable gain of $17,000. If you sold the second block of shares (the February 25 shares), you'll realize a tax loss of $3,000. So which shares did you sell? Some folks might tell you that you can simply come up with an "average" cost for these shares. Don't listen. When it comes to individual stocks, you don't have the choice of "averaging" your cost (you do with mutual funds).

As a rule of thumb, you want to keep your long-term gains intact and use any losses (either short- or long-term) to offset any short-term gains. You receive a preferred tax rate for your long-term capital gains (gains on shares held for more than one year), but you'll pay taxes at your ordinary rate on short-term gains. You really don't want to disturb any of your long-term gains unless you can't help it.

So what should you do? Pay attention to where your gains and losses are coming from and categorize your gains and losses by short-term and long-term components. When possible, try to take short-term losses only against short-term gains. Whenever possible and prudent, allow your long-term gains to be taxed at the preferred tax rate rather than offsetting them with short-term (or even long-term) losses.

## 4. Live Below Your Means

This message perhaps never rings more clearly than when we're in the midst of a recession. Expressed more succinctly, it's just spelled S-A-V-E.

Fellow Fool LouAnn Lofton expressed this well in a recent article for Fool.com:

Do you spend every cent of your paycheck? Is the idea of saving money a joke to you? If so, then pull up a seat. We'd like to introduce you (or perhaps reintroduce you) to the concept of living below your means (LBYM), the concerted effort to save money and spend carefully. Often it involves making sure you get the best possible price for something. Other times, it means evaluating your wants versus your needs and deciding not to spend the money at all.

Why should you bother?

Simple. Because your retirement will need to be financed somehow, and unless you intend to work until you're ninety, it'd be smart to begin planning for it now. Don't you want to be lounging around by the pool with other Fools reading trashy novels in a big floppy hat when you're seventy?

And there are other reasons besides retirement for living below your means. Maybe you have children and you're saving and investing for their college education. Perhaps you're paying off credit card debt and want to cut back in other places so that you have more money each month to put toward becoming debt-free. Any number of reasons can lead you to the conclusion that living frugally and saving and investing money is an intelligent way to live.

At Fool.com, we have an entire discussion board—the "Living Below Your Means" discussion board—dedicated to sharing ideas and advice on the best methods to live below our means. This is the Foolish Mecca for all things fiscally responsible and frugal. Below are some of the most popular tips gleaned from that board. Depending on your perspective, some of these may seem outrageously frugal to you. Others may not seem disciplined enough. It's a motley mix.

1. Start by looking for places in your budget to spend less and save more. One of the most repeated tips in the Fool discussion group is about eating out: Try not to do it too often! Cooking at home can save you tons of money. Along that same vein, take your lunch to work instead of eating out every day. And drink more water—it's cheaper and healthier than soft drinks and fruit juice (hope you didn't think that stuff was healthy for you!). You'll be shocked at how much you aren't spending just by following this first suggestion.

2. Keeping up the maintenance on your car is also a great way to live below your means. Making sure that the brakes work and that the oil's been changed before you smell smoke or hear that grinding noise generally saves you money. In the words of a message board contributor with the screen name of jtesh, "Cherish your belongings. Don't treat everything as a consumable. Take the time to maintain your car; it will last longer and hold its resale value."

3. Shopping at garage sales and thrift stores can save Fools lots of money. You know that old saying about one person's trash is another person's treasure? Uh-huh! Also, when and where you can, buy the generic version of foods at the grocery store. Many times, you won't notice any difference, except for the cheaper price tag. Think about buying in bulk too, from places like Costco or Sam's Club, when and where it makes sense. You can save substantially by doing this, and you'll cut down on your number of trips to the store. Finally, make a shopping list and stick to it!

4. Make a wish list for items that you'd like to buy; implement a waiting period of a few days for your wish list, and honestly examine your wants versus needs. Don't buy anything from your list until the waiting period's up. Try to treat every expense as unaffordable unless you've planned for it. Don't buy on credit, unless you're prepared to pay off your balance every month. Interest charges can make even the most frugal purchase's price skyrocket.

5. Check out places in your budget where you can potentially cut back. Can you bank cheaper? How about your insurance? Get new quotes to see if you can get your current coverage for less. Is your phone service the cheapest possible? Do you really need super-duper-unleaded gas for your car? Would the quality of your life be greatly affected if you no longer had your current cable package—or cable at all? What about that cell phone? Do you really need it? Look carefully at every category in your budget and ask yourself how you can do it for less. In many cases, you'll be able to either cut back an expense, or eliminate it altogether.

6. Another suggestion for saving money (and years on your life) is to quit smoking. One in four Americans smokes today. Gasp. Quitting is a fantastic idea. Not only will you save all that money you've been laying out for ciggies but you'll be literally saving your life as well. Check out the Fool's "Quitting Smoking" discussion board at this Internet address: quitsmoking.Fool.com. Direct your friends there too. It's an amazing place.

7. There are also tons of very specific tips on the LBYM discussion board—things like using fluorescent bulbs and dimmer switches for your lights in order to save energy and money.

Finally, there are a couple of contentious issues with living below your means.

First of all, how much is too much? Sacrifice and deprivation are not synonymous. Try to strike a balance between saving and investing for the future and having a fulfilling life now. Nitpicking over every single last penny will only exhaust you and those around you. It's not worth it to be that stressed out. You could make yourself so unhealthy that you never even reach the retirement you're giving so much up for now.

Charity is another such issue. Should people striving to live below their means set aside money for charity now, or should they just continue to save it all? It's up to each individual or family to decide what's right for them.

Coming up with a budget and learning to live below your means will pay
off in the end. Check out Fool Community online—the most vibrant part
of our Web site—and visit the "Living Below Your Means" discussion
board to share your suggestions or to get advice on your situation from
fellow Fools. Your seventy-year-old self will thank you for it! The board
can be found by typing living below your means in the board search box
at boards.Fool.com.

## 5. Getting Out of Credit Card Debt: The Interest Rate

This timely (for many) suggestion comes to us from fellow
Fool Dayana Yochim, who has an absolute passion for win-
ning back savings from one's creditors. She published this at
Fool.com:

> Lenders use a bafflingly complex system of pulleys, ball bearings, mirrors,
> and Boolean algebra to calculate your finance charge. In the end, most
> come up with a figure somewhere between 0 percent and 32 percent.
>
> Some banks charge a fixed APR (annual percentage rate), which doesn't
> change, while others charge a variable APR that is tied to an index, such
> as the prime rate. The Schumer Box—which must legally be included on
> every credit card solicitation—contains all of a card's vitals. If you can't
> figure out your card's APR by looking at your monthly statement, simply
> call the customer service number for a translation.
>
> Chances are you carry a card that charges interest on the average daily
> balance, which is calculated by adding each month's daily balance and
> dividing that number by the number of days in the month. Many have a
> grace period during which you do not accrue finance charges. If you don't
> pay off your balance in its entirety for each billing period, however, you'll
> accrue interest on new purchases from the day they're posted.
>
> The interest equation takes on labyrinthine proportions when you try to
> figure out whether or not it is based on two months of billing cycles—the
> current and the previous—and the exact length of your grace period.
> Some lenders use an "adjusted balance" method where the previous

month's payment is subtracted and the finance charge is based on the remaining balance.

None of this matters if you pay your balance in full each month—which is exactly what you should do. If you can't pay it off, find a card that excludes new purchases from the interest calculation period.

## PENALTY RATES

Once you've figured out your APR, your lender will probably change it. In fact, credit card companies are not required to notify you in advance before they move the decimals and change the digits. You agreed to let them do so at any time when you signed up for their card.

What raises their ire? Your spending habits, for one. Even if you pay all your bills on time, you may get flagged. Your creditor may look at your credit records every quarter to evaluate the amount of debt relative to the amount of your current income. One recent notice received by a Fool staffer stated that customers could not increase "significantly" the amount they spent on another unsecured card. It defined "significant" as $2,000 or more. Keep your eye on your rates if you plan to make any big purchases.

Your bill-paying habits can also affect your interest rate. If you miss a few payments you could be subject to a penalty rate of up to 32 percent. Ouch. So keep close tabs on when your payment is due.

## TEASER RATES

Like a cotton candy buzz, teaser rates don't last. But they're darn tempting. Creditors are now making it more difficult to continuously transfer balances from one low-interest-rate card to another. If you toss cards aside like wet naps after a rack of barbecued ribs, be prepared to pay a penalty.

Here's a typical scenario: An offer for an eye-poppingly-low-rate card arrives in your mailbox. You jump at the chance to transfer a heap of money you owe to a high-interest card to the new card. After six months, the interest rate on your new card jumps to post-promotional levels— usually in the high teens or low twenties. But you've already got another low-interest lender lined up. You transfer your balance, and, boom! Look out! The dumped card charges you retroactively the higher rate because you didn't read the microscopic print which points out that you cannot transfer a balance for an entire year.

Before you sign up for a card with a low, low interest rate, find out what that rate applies to. Is it new purchases? Cash advances? Balance transfers? Watch out for cards that force you to pay a retroactively higher rate or charge you a penalty fee if you cancel the card. And don't fall for one that expires sooner than six months.

## LOWERING YOUR RATE

If your current lender is charging you more than 12 percent interest, it's time to re-ne-go-ti-ate, Fool. (We mentioned this last chapter, but here's a bit more on it.) Use our Foolish Rate Negotiation Dialogue below to bully your lender into lowering your interest rate.

You: "I just got this incredibly great offer from First Union Banc USA Nation's Edge Choice plan for a Titanium Card with a fixed APR of just 5.9 percent for the rest of my living days! I don't really want to switch cards, your service has been great. But I've noticed that the interest rate you're offering me has crept up to 43.9 percent in the past year. I'm going to have to transfer my balance unless you can lower the interest rate."

Them: (The sound of keyboard tapping and your credit and payment history being scrutinized.)

You: "Did I mention the free toaster?"

Them: (The sound of fake typing as the operator tries to psych you out with silence.)

You: (The sound of you filling out the First Union Banc USA Nation's Edge Choice card application.)

Them: "Uncle! We'd like to keep you as a customer, so I am prepared to lower your interest rate, and waive your annual fee if you choose to stay with us."

At this point they should offer you something around 12 percent if not lower. (You can hold out for the bagel slicer if your daughter's pining for a Barbie doll guillotine.) If you get a dud operator who isn't feeling generous, ask to speak to a supervisor. Granted, if you're perpetually late with your payment, yell at dogs, or litter, your lender may prefer to let you walk. So be prepared to follow through with First Union Banc USA Nation's Edge Choice. But if you have a solid track record with your card, you should have no problem negotiating a lower lending rate.

Another tactic is to remind your lender that he's making money off of you, even if you pay off your balance each month. Credit card companies make 1.3 percent to 2.5 percent from the merchants on every dollar charged. You can use this as leverage to get fees removed and reverse grace period adjustments. Simply keep track of how much you charge each year. When your lender tries to hit you with a $45 annual fee, call and remind them that they got $1,250 per year (or whatever the amount was) in merchant fees, which they won't get next year if you cancel your card. Sit back while the customer service rep grovels.

And now for something completely similar! Via e-mail and discussion board postings, here are some other timely and leading financial suggestions from our online community (with their Motley Fool screen names attached). Read on, you'll be impressed.

### A SIMPLE LIFESTYLE
BY STOKMEISTER

Many here at The Fool online have alluded to a desire or decision to maintain a simple, or frugal lifestyle. As a Quaker, I'm taught to look at the impact of each purchase and consumption, and to examine what it is I really "need" in light of resources available or impact upon the earth.

There is some angst among members of our meetings that wealth creation is, in and of itself, an unnecessary activity, and one that is not compatible with choosing a simple lifestyle. I disagree.

It is my responsibility to work hard and provide for myself and my family. I believe I was born with a set of gifts and talents that should be ed for the betterment of myself, my family, my employer, and my community. Wealth can be accumulated and remain unspent, or it can be allocated. I enjoy giving gifts—and I hope that any money/resources I'm privileged to accumulate can be multiplied by giving back in efforts to help others.

Wealth to some doesn't translate to six, seven, or more figures; but rather in the ability to share our own blessings, no matter how meager.

## I HOPE I TAKE MY OWN ADVICE!
BY GRETCH68

Hi all, here's a suggestion (which I'm really trying to keep in mind myself) that speaks to my goal of doing more to better organize and take active control of my financial situation.

I read a quote recently that has stuck with me as I assess what I need to do regarding my financial future. "He who wants milk should not sit on a stool in the middle of the pasture and expect the cow to back up to him." Basically I interpret this to mean that if I don't actively choose to organize my finances, devoting time to things like budgeting and investment research, then I can't expect things to happen as I'd like them to.

My suggestion is pretty basic and probably totally obvious. It's simply to make a checklist (or lists) of the concrete things you can do or need to do to address priorities or goals, as well as a clear time frame for when they will be done. These things can be as simple as filing bank statements for various accounts in different color folders or spending an hour one or more times a week reading on Fool.com about companies that might be potential investments for an IRA account.

Now a confession. While I preach this kind of organization all the time as a corporate trainer, I don't always take my own advice. Big surprise! In the midst of a busy life, I let go of updating files or tell myself I'm too busy or tired to do my investing homework. Not anymore. I'm going to commit now!

Hopefully someone will find this helpful. Or at the very least, you found the cow quote mildly entertaining? Yes?

BEST SUGGESTION TO IMPROVE FINANCIAL STANDING
BY FAEZ

My suggestion doesn't involve doing something additional, just prioritizing what you're presently doing.

Here's what I mean:

A few years back, I listed all my investments. Checking account, CDs, mutual funds, house (real estate), whatever. I put down the amount that each was worth. Then, next to each one, I estimated the return I was getting. Then put them in order from highest to lowest return. (A spreadsheet is useful for doing this.)

You might be surprised, as was I, that I had the most money invested at the lowest return. And the least invested at the highest return. Now, that might not be a bad thing depending on the situation. And high returns often involve risk. But it stands to be a real eye-opener just to reconsider your decisions. You might be able to reallocate your assets to your advantage.

And similarly, take a look at your debts. That's where you might actually make real progress. List all your debts and the interest rate of each. Put them in order from high to low. Your higher debts should be at the lower interest rates.

You might be amazed that you're paying 19 percent on some credit cards and only 11 percent on some others. Not only that, but you might find that you can consolidate some of that debt into a home equity loan at 7 percent. You might find that putting extra money into paying off your mortgage at 6.5 percent would be better used in paying off credit cards that are charging 19 percent.

Once you've got all your ducks in a row, do something useful with all that money you'll be saving each month. The Vanguard 500 Index Fund might be a good choice.

## EXPECT THE UNEXPECTED

BY EAROGERS

I have not felt the need to be too aggressive financially, as I was in a very secure position and had a long-term plan that would have kept me comfortable had life not taken a sudden and devastating change.

I just turned fifty this year. People have always told me I "look" much younger than my age, and I've also always "felt" younger. Probably, because I didn't have the responsibilities of a husband and kids and because I was an only child with Mom and Dad still living with me and doting on me.

My situation was that in 1990 I designed and had built a four-bedroom home, designed with two distinct and separate living areas so I could move my parents down from Oregon. My father had been in poor health for years after three strokes and additional health problems. My mother was the picture of health, having survived uterine cancer since the mid-1970s. Both retired from Ma Bell just before the split and received excellent benefits and pensions. Between us we could more than afford our lifestyle comfortably. I made the mortgage payments, they paid the utilities (we got free phone service and long distance). I was able to refinance the house a few years ago, so along with paying additional on the principal every month it will be paid off in four years or less. Both my cars are paid off too.

I have a 401(k) from a previous company drawing interest that cannot be added to. It has gone from around $48,000 to $15,000. I contribute about $200 a month to my current 401(k) (which of late is losing more than I'm contributing). I put another $50 per month into a separate fund through my bank's financial services (also lost principal). And I have a money market account.

My plan had been to sit tight until the house was paid off, then take that money and begin contributing it aggressively into investments. This would help me catch up, since I didn't start saving until about twelve years ago. That would give me enough to fulfill my goals to travel often and do fun things with my mother and have enough to afford home care for her when she can no longer care for herself.

Unfortunately, my father died in November 1999. That didn't hurt us much financially. However, my mother died in November 2000, quite suddenly.

So, now things are different. Now I have not only the mortgage to deal with but also all the utilities, taxes, insurance, and upkeep of this house, the cars, and yard. The financial burden is challenging enough but I am unfortunately "domestically challenged." My mother was in effect my housekeeper. She took care of everything from cleaning to maintenance.

So now, just getting through the next four years will be the challenge. I don't want to stop making the extra principal payments and I don't want to take anything out of any of the savings/investment accounts. Due to some recent car repairs, expenses of a vacation that was planned a year ago, and some outstanding debts of my mother's, I've incurred some credit card debt that cannot be paid off at the end of the month. However, I've been able to take advantage of introductory 0 percent offers to transfer the balance from one card to another and think I'll be able to pay it off in installments before the 0 percent rate expires.

I also readjusted my mutual fund allocation to increase the amount in bonds and decrease the stock fund until things pick up. My bond funds are the only ones that have not shown a negative through this whole downturn. Hopefully, they'll make up the difference in the stock losses, short-term, so I can at least begin to break even.

I've never been comfortable putting money into single stocks. With mutual funds you usually have enough stock in "good" companies to offset any "bad" companies, so there's less risk, even with an aggressive fund.

I don't like managing, monitoring, or researching. But I also don't want to pay someone big bucks to manage for me, with no guarantee I won't still invest in a loser and also be out the money to the financial manager. So, I'm here hoping that light bulbs will flash, giving me insights on how best to recoup my current losses and cover myself in the future.

As I await that enlightenment, my suggestion to all readers of this note is simple. Prepare in advance. As best you can, prepare for the unexpected. The more you do, the happier you'll be when the unexpected strikes (which for each of us, in its own way, it will).

## REFLECTIONS ON INSURANCE
### BY FOOLBERT1

My best suggestion has to do with insurance, in particular long-term-care insurance. I'll start by strongly recommending to those who don't have it, get it.

First, what is it? It's insurance for care that an individual may require as a result of accident, injury, or chronic long-term illness. This can be nursing home care, home health care, and custodial care.

Second, why would you need it? Because people are living longer, nursing home care costs are rising, and children may be unable financially to care for their parents.

Third, okay, if you need long-term care, and you don't have it, what are you relying on . . .

> 1. Paying the cost yourself. In 1997, the average cost was more than $46,000 per year for nursing home care, and the average length of stay was two and a half years.

> 2. Relying on Medicare. Medicare pays only for skilled care, and only for a limited period of time.

> 3. Depending on Medicaid. In order to qualify for Medicaid, an individual is required to spend down all assets to the point of poverty. Medicaid will then assume the cost of long-term care. However, the individual has by that time forfeited all right of choice.

None of these options strikes me as particularly ideal. For this reason, I've locked down long-term-care insurance.

# 8
# Rebuilding with Perspective

Buy when everyone else is selling, and hold until everyone else is buying. This is not merely a catchy slogan. It is the very essence of successful investment.

—J. PAUL GETTY

We've just reviewed our situations and effectively asked, "What can we do differently?" and "How can we think differently?" about our financial lives. Building off our Ideal Selves, it's now time, forevermore, to view ourselves as investors. Let's put that in bigger type size:

## investors!

You better believe it. Investors in homes. Investors in health. Investors in the stock market. Investors in education. Investors in insurance. Investors in food. Investors in our own entertainment. Investors throughout our entire budget, asking ourselves, "Am I getting more than what I'm paying for?" What a key question that is. Making a habit of answering it when you open your wallet is the first step toward permanent financial independence and security. You may be thinking,

"Well, then, I've never seen an investment I didn't like." But, c'mon, if you really ask yourself that key question, "Am I actually getting more value than I'm paying?" we suggest that more often than you expect, your answer will be, "No—this isn't worth it. It isn't worth my time and effort and money. I won't make this investment."

The same question, dear Fool, holds true when you invest in the stock market. Remember that out of 10,000 publicly traded companies, the 500 largest make up more than 85 percent of the total value of the stock market. Five percent of all the companies out there account for virtually all public-market value. Truly, the majority of public companies are not worth your time, effort, or money.

Perhaps, though, you're not even thinking of investing in stocks. Maybe last time through, you got in at the wrong time and out at the wrong time. Your fingertips are burned or broken. You're hanging your head. You think you'll never be able to forget, and never again be able to equal, how much money you had back in March 2000. Naturally, then, you have little interest in reengaging and reinvesting.

On top of that, it's hard to know where our markets are headed. Is our path unpaved, tortuous, littered with hairpin turns? Does the next earnings warning or major corporate bankruptcy lurk a moment off? Will Kmart even be around by next year? Will Xerox? Or can we expect, soon enough, to skip happily down a sunlit road of rising and unprecedented corporate profits? As usual, the reality's likely to be somewhere between the two. But if we take a look at history, we can't help but gain confidence in our decisions and even capitalize on new opportunities (yes, opportunities).

## OUR UNCERTAIN TIMES

By the end of 2001, we were living in strange times—fighting a war in Afghanistan, a country that hated its own leaders; absorbing bomb threats and anthrax scares at home; recovering from the worst terrorist attack in the history of our country.

And we are certainly still in uncertain times. The past year provided plenty of examples. Who would've imagined the bankruptcies of Polaroid and Bethlehem Steel? Who could've thought the CEO of United Airlines would declare that, absent changes in the economic climate, his airline would go Chapter 11 as well (and then quit two weeks later)?

The business markets are, by nature, unpredictable. In fact, there's more uncertainty in business right now than at any point over the past quarter century. If you've been investing long enough, you know of that familiar and accurate claim: The stock market hates uncertainty. But are we really in a situation largely without precedent? Of course we are. When you think about it, there is, thankfully, no precedent. The terrorist attacks on September 11 destroyed the lives of thousands of people, brought down twin icons of American commerce, hit at the heart of our defense network, and resulted in direct financial costs in excess of $30 billion.

But when we're trying to figure out what the future might hold for the economy and the market, we can still look to history to provide us with at least some context and guidance. Not guarantees, not absolutes—just context and guidance. Let's look again at how the market (and, by proxy, the economy) has reacted in the past to various conflicts and events.

## MARKET COMPARISONS

Calamity and disaster in America have customarily been followed by opportunity and reward. In the six months following each listed crisis, the stock market enjoyed a double-digit rise:

| | |
|---|---|
| Cuban Missile Crisis | + 24% |
| Assassination of John F. Kennedy | + 15% |
| Richard Nixon's Resignation | + 13% |
| 1987 Market Crash | + 15% |
| Declaration of the Gulf War | + 19% |
| Oklahoma City Bombing | + 33% |

And from each of these, the market rose to greater heights in the decade to follow. In fact, over no decade in the past 100 years in America has the stock market failed to make gains. While we won't claim the inevitability of the recurrence of this pattern, that's a compelling statistic.

More specific to the terrorist attacks and the war, we find three comparisons to the attacks of September 11. First, as an act of war. Second, as an act of terrorism. And third, as a natural disaster—since this approximates the massive burden shouldered by insurance companies.

If we're talking war, let's start with the Japanese attack on Pearl Harbor in December of 1941:

- In the six months that followed the attack, the Dow was down 10 percent.

- The S&P 500 declined almost 17 percent in the five months following Pearl Harbor.

- Two years after Pearl Harbor, though, the Dow was up 28.2 percent.

- By the time World War II ended in 1945, the S&P had risen 62 percent from its December 1941 level.

The market also wavered but eventually rose after the 1990 invasion of Kuwait by Iraq:

- Starting on August 2, 1990, the day of the attack, the S&P 500 declined over the next three months by 11.3 percent.

- The Dow dropped almost 9 percent in the month after the attack.

- A year later, the S&P was 10.6 percent higher.

- Two years after the invasion, the Dow was up 18.5 percent.

What about the market's performance following previous terrorist attacks in this country?

- After the first World Trade Center attack in 1993, the Dow fell 0.5 percent the day of the bombing, then climbed more than 2 percent over the next month and was up 8 percent after six months.

- In reaction to the 1995 bombing of the Murrah Federal Building in Oklahoma, the Dow was up 3 percent the month after the attack and up 14 percent over the next six months.

While the aforementioned terrorist events were horrific, the attacks on September 11 were much worse in terms of lives lost and property destroyed. Nevertheless, investors must note what has repeatedly happened in the past: namely, recovery in the midst of pessimism. Let's dig deeper and look at previous market reactions to natural disasters that caused extensive damage:

- Hurricane Andrew in 1992 is currently the most expensive disaster in the history of the U.S. It caused an estimated $20 billion to $25 billion in damages. The Dow rose slightly in the sessions following the hurricane and finished up 4 percent after six months.

- After the 1994 earthquake in Los Angeles, which caused $15 billion in damage and $10 billion in lost output, the Dow rose slightly in the days following the quake, but fell 1.7 percent over the next six months.

It's hard to say exactly where among these reactions we should place the awful events of September 11. We aren't in a conventional war. The attacks have no comparison in our past, and it seems unlikely that the market will process the events as it has natural disasters. Still, we can gain some perspective from the above data: Our free markets are very, very resilient and prone to rise over time in anticipation of gradual improvements.

## THE BIG "R"

Let's consider what has happened to the stock market during recessions. (A debatable but commonly accepted definition of recession is two successive quarters of a decline in the GDP—gross domestic product.) Starting in March 2001, we fell into recession. The early signs were there. Consumer confidence was waning. Corporate profits were suffering. The Nasdaq was down more than 50 percent from its highs in March 2000. The layoffs continued apace. Then between September 11 and the end of 2001, U.S. corporations laid off more than 500,000 employees. This past year has marked historic rounds and numbers of layoffs in the U.S.

To stem the tide, the Federal Reserve cut interest rates eleven times in 2001, dropping them to their lowest levels in more than forty years. Okay, so what can we learn from past recessions?

Since World War II, there have been nine recessions. And there have been nine recoveries. Despite the recessions, and other periods of great uncertainty for our country—the Cuban Missile Crisis, the assassination of JFK, the Watergate scandal, the oil crisis, double-digit inflation, and the bizarre over-demand for Cabbage Patch Kids—the American economy, built on open competition and relatively light government intervention (cf. Japan as a counterexample), has been vibrant.

Since World War II, corporate earnings are up sixty-three-fold and the stock market's up seventy-one-fold. In other words, the market has rebounded from each and every recession we've faced in the preceding half century. Recessions themselves are even becoming milder, lasting on average around one year. Conversely, market recoveries have lasted, on average, between four and eight years. So it's worth noting that for more than fifty years, investing straight through a recession has been good investor policy. Obviously, increasing investments in the middle of a recession has made even better sense.

## EVERYTHING AND NOTHING

Our perspective, then, is that everything has changed and nothing's changed. Everything has changed because our lives will never return to pre–September 11 innocence. We'll get used to being more vigilant, more cautious, and more patient. We'll find new security measures taken around us, and maybe even take on a few ourselves. We'll never forget the attacks of September 11. But when we talk about investing, and all other aspects of our money, arguably nothing material has changed.

- You should still be taking action toward crafting the Ideal You.

- Our tenet of not having money invested in the market that you'll need in less than five years still holds.

- Not letting the day-to-day fluctuations affect your financial decisions is still core to our approach.

- Using indexing (of equities and bonds when appropriate) as the backbone of your mutual fund investments still makes sense to us. (More to come about index funds in Chapter 9.)

- Investing only in companies 1) that you believe will be around and generating greater profit in ten years, 2) whose products and services you know well, and 3) that you track against the market's average return makes sense to us too.

What, then, do we think you should do regarding your long-term savings?

Not to be glib, but again, you should start with reflection. The long-term investment picture for you shouldn't have changed on September 11. Clearly, a mistaken action to take was to panic and sell. A slightly different mistake you could have made, in our opinion, is to sell intentionally in hopes of perfectly timing the market. The data suggests that's a terrible risk to take. If you'd missed the best forty months of the last forty years in the stock market, your return would have dropped from 11 percent to 3 percent per year. Ooof. Rather than doubling your money every six and a half years, your stock market investments would have doubled every twenty-four years, outpaced by inflation!

We know that it's difficult to think about the long term when we face grim horrors and the road ahead seems dark. We're not here to say, "Don't worry; the economy will recover this quarter." Rather, the road ahead may not be easy going for some time yet. So, marshal your resources and prepare to weather even more pain. Remember, though, that the nine recessions since World War II have led to nine recoveries. Some of the very best times to add long-term money to your stock portfolio have been smack in the middle of those recessions.


## SEEING THINGS AS THEY ARE

Clearly, we cannot be our Ideal Selves unless we regularly review our stock and mutual fund portfolio decisions. The completion of this review requires consideration of our past performance, an ability to see things as they are, and paying attention to mapping out our future. Let's get started with the worst, first.

Our mistakes.

My, how it can be frustrating to sort through our mistakes. Sickening, in fact. Enough to roll the stomach twice, go green in the face, dread the morning light, wave off the chicken soup, and splay ourselves out on the sofa, a terrible mess. But facing our mistakes and taking lessons from them is the first step toward a life without financial anxiety. Tackling this stuff in times of upheaval and disappointment is what will actually secure your early retirement, fund your kids through college, solidify a career change, help you to claim that whitewashed house on Juniper Lane.

Thus, the spirit of our effort here is in the interests of planning for longevity, opportunity, security, and adventure. Of course, for those of us who believe investing in the stock market is an essential key to our financial plans, volatility has become almost a way of life. As of this writing, it is now the twentieth month of our discontent. Back on March 24, 2000, the S&P 500 index traded at a high of 1,552. Today, the index of 500 very large, primarily U.S.-based companies is scrambling around 1,050, marking a 32 percent decline from its peak.

The Nasdaq has fallen further still. Its accelerated decline matches in distance, though not duration, the devastatingly slow decline of the Japanese stock market. The Naz touched its all-time high on March 10, 2000. Back then, all manner of companies that are today in bankruptcy, or verging on it, were valued in the billions of dollars (eToys, @Home, CMGI et al.). Then the switch flipped. This past September, the Nasdaq dipped below 1,500. Nasdaq investors had suffered a brain-rattling 72 percent drop.

If you're a stock investor, as are we, your patience and your durability are fiercely being tested. One downtick leads to the next. One profit warning swells to three. The talk's been of recession, a possible depression, and a forty years' war. Financial pundits muse on staple budgeting and the collapse of consumer confidence. The halls of our public marketplace have grown dim. The candles hiss.

And so even with all the reason and simplicity of Mr. Getty's quotation that opened this chapter, it's damned difficult to abide. We can't fathom profiting when war is upon us. We can't fathom buying into distress, buying when the house is abandoned. We can't imagine buying rain and selling into sunshine. But among others, renowned investor Warren Buffett has always challenged those who would listen to do just that. Relevant Buffett quotes for today's investor (and for any day's investor) abound. How about these:

"Be fearful when others are greedy and greedy only when others are fearful."

"Great investment opportunities come around when excellent companies are surrounded by unusual circumstances that cause the stock to be misappraised."

Certainly, few of us are feeling greedy today. It can be hard
to imagine even getting our portfolios back to where they
once were. No doubt, if you're a stock investor, some of your
holdings have fallen 30 percent, 50 percent, 70 percent, some
more. Even Mr. Buffett's Berkshire Hathaway is 10 percent
below where it was two and a half years ago.

But if you're hanging your head, you're probably not hanging it as low as Warren Buffett's mentor, Benjamin Graham,
hung his after being virtually wiped out in the Great Depression. Distraught, Graham redoubled his intellectual effort, developing a financial approach of enduring excellence that is
revered by millions of investors. This is the time to make that
effort with your money. To rethink your assumptions. To redouble your efforts.

It may be hard to renew your enthusiasm for investment re-
thinking. Some of us may not have the time nor intellectual energy to remain engaged. Others may have been stunned by
their lack of financial preparedness. Still others may have lost
sight of the fact that the last five years in the U.S. market have
actually been highly average. From November 1996 to November 2001, the stock market has now risen at a rate of just about
10 percent per year. That's one percentage point below the average annual returns for stock investors this past century.

So today, with the stocks of steadily profitable and well-
heeled companies like Microsoft, eBay, and Starbucks off
more than 50 percent, should we not renew our enthusiasm
for building our portfolio? With the general stock market—
which historically doubles every six and a half years—down
more than 30 percent, should we not increase our appetite for
401(k) investments? Certainly, we should at least consider it.
Not blindly. Not hastily. Not fanatically. But with the S&P 500
down 30 percent, we absolutely should be more enthusiastic
about stocks and stock mutual funds.

## TAKE ACTION

Like any other talk in this section, we're prepared to help you back it up with meaningful action. Here are three steps you can use to proceed forward with your investments—money put away to grow:

1. What do you have? As you're working on creating the Ideal You, take stock in your investments and remind yourself what you are holding in all of those accounts. Gather up those statements and create a working list for yourself. List all of the mutual funds (including index funds), individual stocks, and bonds that you own. If you are feeling adventurous, indicate how much you have of each.

2. Take a deep breath and determine how you feel about what you see. Our perspective is that your trust and confidence should remain intact during this time, but what do you think? Answer these questions:

- Have your assumptions about the market changed?
- Have your assumptions changed about any investments you've made?
- What actions will you take based on these new assumptions?
- Might now be the time to get aggressive about saving and investing?

3. Begin to redouble your efforts. We'll be looking at some specific buying opportunities next chapter, but we're pretty sure a few of you are looking at your portfolios, wondering about the stuff you already have. Determining when to sell is one of the toughest issues for investors. There aren't many rules that apply to every investor and every mutual fund or stock in every situation. Don't worry—all's not lost. We've got some guidance for you. Here are a bunch of situations in which you should consider selling some stock:

- The reasons you bought are no longer valid.
- You can't remember why you bought it in the first place.
- You don't know what the company does and how it makes money.
- The stock has become significantly overvalued relative to your fair-value price, if you have one.
- You'll need the money within just a few years.
- You've found a much more attractive place to invest your money.
- You're only hanging on for emotional reasons.
- You've lost confidence in the company.
- You hold too many stocks.
- You hold too few stocks.

When evaluating mutual funds, look for funds that are able to beat the S&P 500. If your funds aren't, then you might be better off in an index fund. An index fund is a passively managed fund that seeks to match the performance of a particular market index.

This doesn't mean that you sell automatically. There are a number of ill effects you could suffer from selling your funds, such as capital gains taxes and triggering backend loads or redemption fees. Make sure you analyze all the costs before selling your funds. For those interested in further consideration and action, we have an online seminar entitled "Pick the Best Mutual Funds" that provides you a step-by-step approach if you're really thinking of dumping some of those funds. It is available in our online store at Foolmart.com in our seminar department.

Over long periods of time, we think it's very hard for professionally managed mutual funds to beat a total market index fund. This should get you thinking about whether it's time to reassess your holdings and be ready to jump into some of the tax consequences of selling.

# 9

# Five, No, *Six* Investments for the Future

No man is so foolish but he may sometimes give another good counsel, and no man so wise that he may not easily err if he takes no other counsel than his own. He that is taught only by himself has a fool for a master.

—BEN JONSON

In our consideration of the present day, What to Do Now, we're nearing the final bend and heading for the stretch together. This chapter, and then some interactive Q&A with Qs from more of our online community voices, close out the race to understand *what to do now*. Here in Chapter 9 we'd like to share what we consider to be six relatively timely and timeless investment ideas.

As ever, The Motley Fool doesn't want you to shut off your brain, listen up, and do as we say. No drones allowed. You know your individual situation better than we do, so you're far more likely to know what's right for you. And, of course, *you're* the final judge in all your financial matters. We just hope our thoughts can help you make better decisions. Without further ado, six investment ideas.

## 1. Certificates of Deposit (CDs)

Certificates of deposit are federally insured instruments for your *short-term savings.* By that we mean any money that you might need for emergencies. We also mean any money that you'll definitely need for expenses over the next three to five years. Do you have annual mortgage payments? Car loans? Credit card debt payments? Have you committed to paying for Allie to go to the college of her choice soon? All these are examples of expenditures that'll use up *short-term money.*

The stock market is no place for that capital. Obviously, stocks are too darned unpredictable. From peak to trough, the Nasdaq fell more than 70 percent between March 2000 and September 2001. That's our lifetime reminder that the short-term risk of owning equities is substantial (please pass this learning on to children and grandchildren). Over just a few years, $100,000 can fall to $30,000. Or $12,000 could drop to $3,000. Or $3.9 million may narrow to $1.2 million. It can happen. *It just did happen.* So, please, think this aspect of your financial plan through carefully.

That does *not* mean, however, that you must settle for weak passbook savings rates. Take a look at CDs and their interest rates. CDs have a specific maturity, ranging from three months to five years. (If you want a good rate for point of comparison, MBNA—a partner of The Motley Fool—offers special rates on CDs for Fools. Drop by the Fool's Savings Center at savings.Fool.com for details.)

Two important things to remember about CDs.

First, you can't get your money out of a CD before its maturity date without paying a penalty. For a CD to be effective, you'll need clarity on how long you can put away the money. Second, obviously CDs aren't going to make you rich. At rates of 5 percent per year, your money would increase 28 percent in five years. At those rates, it would take more than fourteen years to double that money (twice longer than through the historical returns for stocks). But we're talking here about your *short-term savings*—anything you'll need in the next five years. Trying to get rich on your short-term savings invites high risk and disaster.

## 2. A Cheap Broad–Market Index Fund

Our second idea ushers in our old friend the index fund. We think it merits our tireless affection. Why? Because it's a simple, cost-effective, mind-relaxing way to earn solid equity rates of return.

An index fund gives every investor (of small or large portfolios) the ability to invest in thousands of publicly traded companies in America. From a performance standpoint, the beauty and truth of the index fund is that you'll outperform the majority of mutual funds run by overpaid investment portfolio managers. (Guess who overpays them? The fundholders.)

Let's make sure we all know what an index fund is.

An index is a vehicle for tracking a particular group of investments. We'll mention two very, very large indices. The first is the Standard & Poor's 500, an index of 500 of the leading companies trading on the U.S. stock markets. The second is the Wilshire 5000, which tracks the compiled performance of over 6,000 (as it turns out) American businesses today.

An index fund purchases all of the stocks listed on that index. Among our favorites is Vanguard's Total Stock Market Index Fund, a mutual fund that replicates the Wilshire 5000. It therefore purchases ownership in thousands of different companies. In so doing, the fund simply duplicates the overall stock market's yearly gains (or losses). In other words, you're just earning the stock market's average return with this fund.

If getting *average* returns doesn't sit you up in your chair and put a silly smile on your face, well, try this on for size. Over 90 percent of all actively managed mutual funds have done worse than the passively managed Total Stock Market Index Fund over the past ten years. And the great majority of brokers, advisors, money managers, and the like don't do as well as the market average, either.

How could this be? How could so many pros lose?

Well, index funds are far more cost-effective than what the

professionals offer. Actively managed mutual funds bring high salaries, high commission fees, and high taxes from active trading. All get charged against *your* account. Conversely, index funds have very low operating expenses and transaction costs. Why? Because an index fund simply buys and holds a particular index of stocks. Because of that, indexing is both extremely tax-efficient and low in fees. Vanguard's index funds carry an expense ratio (the percentage of the fund's assets that go directly toward the expense of running the fund) of about 0.20 percent. Compare that to the 1.45 percent per year fee of the average mutual fund, which is extremely tax-*inefficient* and which typically underperforms the market's average. These funds charge a yearly expense ratio more than seven times higher than the index fund. Astonishing, really.

Vanguard was the pioneer in indexing. It offered the Vanguard S&P 500 Index Fund back in 1976. No one had before proposed that mutual funds could be *passively* managed. Many simply didn't believe that indexing could gain in popularity. After all, who would want *mediocre* returns? They laughed off the index fund. But it turns out that being average on the stock market is well above average. Vanguard's 500 Fund, as well as its Total Stock Market Index Fund, are two of the largest mutual funds in the world today.

We recommend both of them because there is actually very little difference between them. The S&P 500 represents 85 percent of the total stock market's value. So the difference between Vanguard's 500 Index Fund and its Total Stock Market Index Fund is negligible. That said, we slightly lean toward the Total Stock Market Index Fund because of the breadth of its holdings.

To learn more, read up at www.vanguard.com. Other companies offer similar index funds, by the way. Just make sure you know what you're indexing, and that your annual fees are less than one half of one percent.

## 3. The Bond Index Fund

Our third investment idea is also an indexing idea. It was also pioneered by Vanguard. This time, though, instead of indexing equities, we're talking about indexing bonds. Bond index funds are just as cost-effective as stock index funds. Vanguard showcases four bond index funds: the Vanguard Total Bond Market Index Fund, as well as three others categorized by the length to maturity of the bonds they're invested in.

Why are we suggesting bonds?

While we can't say enough about the *long-term* benefits of investing in stocks, still, it's critical for you to assess your own temperament and to know your time horizon. As your time horizon changes and your investment goals change (both are inevitable), your capital allocation should change as well. Thus, as you near retirement, it's prudent to shift some of your long-term stock investments out of the market and into more conservative vehicles. If one of your investment goals is to provide money for Junior's Ivy League education in seven years, and the second is to be ready for your retirement two years after that, it'd be smart to move some of your savings into a bond fund.

Why? For the same reason we suggested keeping short-term savings out of the stock market. The less time you have before you need the money, the less time available to you to withstand a market hit. So, meet your new conservative friend, the bond index fund. Remember that owning bonds is like owning loans to corporations and other organizations. For this reason, the rates of return are considerably more conservative and predictable.

Vanguard's bond index funds are equal in efficiency and cost-effectiveness to their stock index funds. They carry annual expense ratios in the 0.2 percent to 0.3 percent range. From the standpoint of performance, the universe of bond mutual funds is quite like that of stock mutual funds. Between 1988 and 1998, bond index funds returned 8.9 percent annually versus the 8.2 percent returned by actively managed bond funds. Another ringing endorsement for *not* buying managed mutual funds.

Only you can determine the right mix in your own portfolio between stocks and bonds. A bond index fund, though, is an easy and efficient way to get the income and safety of the bond market without trying to pick out individual bonds your-self. For your shorter-term money (two years), consider Van-guard's Short-Term Bond Index Fund. For your mid-term money (five years), consider Vanguard's Intermediate-Term Bond Index Fund.

## 4. Philip Morris and Dividends

For some, the thought of owning the bond market in the years ahead isn't appetizing. Lending your money, when in-terest rates are at forty-year lows, hardly sets your heart afire.

Welcome to the stage, Philip Morris (soon to be called the Altria Group, Inc., though we'll probably still prefer "Flip Mo"). Philip Morris sells Marlboro, Virginia Slims, and Merit cigarettes, as well as Miller Genuine Draft, Milwaukee's Best, and Foster's lager beers. The company, along with its public-market food subsidiary, Kraft, does more than $80 billion in annual sales and $8 billion in yearly profit.

When it's doing business right, Philip Morris markets its to-bacco and alcohol products exclusively to adults. By law, adults bear the responsibility, through clear disclaimers, of knowing the negative effects of tobacco and alcohol. Philip Morris is plenty justified to sell into this market. However, when Philip Morris is doing business wrong, it markets to un-derage minors—an action that has caused grief and had severe financial costs for the company and industry over the years. It now appears, though, that Philip Morris will weather the legal storm.

Investors looking for the relatively conservative returns and income of bonds would do well to look at Philip Morris's div-idend yield of 5 percent today. Philip Morris stock has appre-ciated significantly over the past eighteen months. But the company still: 1) generates more than $2 billion in cash per quarter, 2) doles out a bondlike annual dividend, and 3) is un-likely to see declining demand for its addictive products any time soon. Any stock price appreciation supplements that very high dividend. Obviously, for some—perhaps for many—the ethical issues of owning shares of this business are a sticking point. For us, as long as the company is forthright, and markets and sells products to consenting adults, they are sufficiently ethical. Whether they're selling to just adults, though, is open to debate.

We must add, however, that we very much believe that your investment dollars should follow your own tastes, beliefs, and *actions* in life. What is "socially responsible" for one person is not for another. We are all different. For someone who smokes, we consider Flip Mo a perfectly good choice for an investment. For someone who is opposed to smoking, we would suggest you invest your dollars elsewhere; just as you don't support the company's products, we think you shouldn't support their stock, either.

We don't smoke, and we don't actually own this stock. But we want to make it clear first and foremost that your investments should generally mirror who you are, how you spend your time, and what you believe in. For a more in-depth presentation of our opinions on socially responsible investing, including what we sometimes call "socially *irresponsible* mutual funds," you can check out that chapter in our starter guide *You Have More Than You Think*.

## 5. Starbucks

From bonds and dividend yields to coffee—such is the mind of a Fool. But we won't talk about just any old coffee company as our number five investment idea. No, we're sticking to the mack daddy of coffee, the king of cappuccino, the mother of mocha, the lord of the latte.

What's so attractive about Starbucks? To start, it's an especially pointed example of Peter Lynch–like thinking for many of us. In fact, it goes one step further. Why settle for just buying what you know—Lynch's classic maxim—when instead you can buy what you *absolutely must have every morning lest you chew off someone's ear in an argument at the office?*

You get the drift.

We all know Starbucks. Most of us recognize the green mermaid signage. Coffee drinkers know they can find a Starbucks in the airport for preflight sipping. Many like being able to pick up a consistent brand of latte clear across the country (and, in select cases, across the world). And who doesn't like the little brown cardboard grabbers that protect consumers from burnt palms?

But that's hardly enough to make for a great investment. So let's look at some data. The company's been around since the 1970s and is currently on an unprecedented (for a coffee brand) worldwide growth spree. Its sales grew 22 percent in 2001, with same-store sales increasing 5 percent. It anticipates growing revenues by 25 percent *per year* through 2005. And, over the last year, Starbucks upped its international reach by 77 percent. Today, fully 20 percent of Starbucks stores are overseas. The company hopes to have 650 shops in Europe alone by the end of fiscal 2003.

The company has no debt, and while its growth is dependent upon new store successes (and especially success overseas), it's also been able to maintain strong same-store sales growth. The comparisons are even more impressive given that, in sum, most retailers had an absolutely horrid 2001. Starbucks, though, managed to eke out a 1 percent sales gain in the tragic month of September 2001, when retail sales nationwide slipped a nasty 2.4 percent.

There's no way to say for sure which companies will thrive in the coming years and which ones won't. Starbucks, though, in our opinion, has all the hallmarks of a champ: strong brand, must-have (addictive?) product, fantastic sales growth, no debt, and room to grow (after all, coffee is the second most consumed liquid on the planet, behind water). We think Starbucks over the long term is a market-beater.

## 6. Manage Your Portfolio for Life

Would we really close this chapter without a more general point? Certainly not. Our teaching aims are broad. The best advice we can give is to create financial plans that: 1) inspire you to stay financially involved throughout life, and 2) play to your intellectual interests (a more dynamic portfolio if you're deeply fascinated by finance; a total market index fund if you're fascinated by just about everything but finance).

A great recent disappointment for us is to hear of investors who've simply tossed in the towel on thinking about their money, after a terrible year for equities. We feel strongly that the time in life given over to saving and investing should be largely a source of joy, and at the very least a neutral experience for you (even during the tough years). If you keep working at it—even when you're disappointed by the immediate reward, even if you're frightened by recent substantial declines on paper—you'll be rewarded. Any individual year may eat at you, but any individual decade is likely to warm your heart.

Please, *manage your portfolio for life.*

From the standpoint of saving, this means eliminating credit card debt. It means aiming to set aside 10 percent plus of your annual salary (whatever you can swing), alongside the gradual elimination of other debts. From the standpoint of investing, it means allocating your money according to time horizon (one to five years, CDs and bonds; five to ten years, primarily stocks; ten years or more, heavily stocks). And it means allocating your money according to your interest and temperament. We suggest indexing but with a focus on individual bonds and stocks if you're deeply fascinated with finance. Only mildly interested? Perhaps 50 percent to 90 percent indexing, then, with some individual bonds or stocks. And 100 percent indexing if you don't have any interest in this book besides the jokes and stories.

# 10

# Your Questions, Our Answers

**Every clarification breeds new questions.**

—ARTHUR BLOCK

The Motley Fool, in case you haven't noticed, serves as a recruiter and facilitator of great talent: yours! From just a handful of visitors our first day of online business in 1994, we rose to 2.5 million Fools using our Web site by the end of 2001. When you consider that that number is actually *up* over the course of a truly abysmal stock market, you'll see why we're excited to come to work every day.

Clearly, many of us are drawn to Fool.com not for "hot stock tips" (very few have existed in recent memory) but something more enduring, something deeper: a desire to make better financial decisions across all categories of our lives. That's where our company comes in, bringing a love of plain talk and wit to our very important subject. But again . . . whose wit? Often, yours! We're privileged to interact and learn from so many of you every day at Fool.com, primarily through our community discussion boards. The mutual reward is to know that our mutual efforts improve one another's lives, and every person we help to get out of debt or to reclaim his or her assets from some mediocre, high-fee manager truly makes the world a better place.

Which is all a long way of saying that we love to interact with our readers—exactly why we wanted to reserve two chapters in this section for doing just that. Chapters 10 and 11 represent the ongoing conversation between readers and Fool HQ, since as you can see we have taken a slew of questions regarding What to Do Now. Consequently, these are rich and long chapters. We hope you enjoy every single Q&A, but those with less time or inclination can skim through and find whatever most suits their fancy, before pushing on to "What Next?"

Please note that not every question under the sun will appear here. If you're particularly curious about a question of your own, we encourage you to visit us. Come to Fool.com and register for a free thirty-day trial membership to our community.

**Q: We all have learned a lot in the past two years. As an investor, how different are you now? Are you going to make any significant changes in the way you are going to invest in the future?**

Particularly in response to the events of September 11, we're all the time hearing these days about how "everything has changed forever." Presumably one's investment approach too, eh? And yet we think this whole emphasis on how "everything has forever changed" is overblown. Why? *Because the only constant IS change.* Hey now, *of course* everything is forever changed—that's a daily ritual and reality that we only miss if we're not paying attention. Most of us are changing in numerous infinitesimal ways every single day, as we live and learn and mature and screw up etc. etc.—you get the point. The same is true of your investment approach. We hope you didn't think you knew it all when the market reached its top in early 2000. And we hope you don't think you know absolutely nothing useful now, following two consecutive dispiriting years for investors. This is just a bear market. Stocks go down for a while. It's happened six times during our first thirty-five years on this planet, and it'll happen probably six times more in the next thirty-five years.

Here's the right mentality: Your investment approach and portfolio, in whatever form, should forever be open to your scrutiny—eternally open books. Indeed, even if you'd thought you had the perfect approach to investing today and wished forever just to maintain it, guess what? The world would change on you. All of a sudden, if you didn't keep your eyes open, you would lose money while many others make it because of fundamental shifts in technology and the marketplace. If you're going to be a self-directed stock market investor, you must be prepared to adapt. (You'll recall our comparison of business to evolution.)

So there's a Golden Mean between not overreacting and not adapting at all. For our own part, we're going to continue focusing on buying and holding good companies, but with two stronger emphases: 1) making sure we really really really (hope we're emphasizing this enough) *really* feel comfortable in our knowledge of the company, so that we don't buy any more JDS Uniphase, for instance, just because "optical networking" seems to be where the world is headed, and 2) we're going to readjust our expectations lower in terms of the returns we're *expecting*. For several years going, we were making 25 percent plus annually, and in fact one year our Rule Breaker Portfolio at Fool.com pulled in a 199 percent return. That was a once-in-a-lifetime year, and five consecutive years of 20 percent plus returns took 100 years to happen and probably will not happen again for at least 100 years more. For a while, there, we were highly insistent that we would only invest our money if we could see it multiplying quickly. That's addictive and unrealistic. We're quite comfortable with stocks showing 10 percent returns annually, because it's a darned sight better than most other things out there.

We both have been investing for seventeen and fifteen years respectively, but we don't regard our combined thirty-two years of experience as much more than just a prelude to the next thirty-two years, full of equally challenging and often different decisions—but continuing to reward disciplined risk taking and investment in companies that you truly understand. And let us also emphasize the importance of having fun through good markets and bad. But that's for the final chapter.

**Q: I read articles and comments from Warren Buffett suggesting that the market is still overvalued. What about this market being overvalued?**

At last check, Buffett still had billions of dollars invested in the stock market. We feel comfortable with our less-than-billions invested, as well. There are always undervalued, underappreciated companies in every single market. Though certainly there are periods where the overall market is too richly priced. But like Peter Lynch, we don't believe in timing the stock market overall. If you're a stock market investor, find good companies and invest in them.

**Q: Won't the fact that so many baby boomers will be retiring at the same time, needing cash flow from their investments, cause the market to drop in value?**

This notion has been popularized by the author Harry Dent (*The Roaring 2000s,* etc.). It has demographic validity, certainly, but we're not so sure about economic validity. You see, the money that baby boomers will remove from the market still gets spent, right? It doesn't just vanish. It will be spent on businesses, and those businesses will have greater profits to show for it, more likely to attract additional investors' money. If you want to adopt this Dent premise, we would only suggest that it won't lead to any Grand Crash, but may redirect capital into certain industries that serve seniors (pharmaceuticals, biotechnology, and online services), while removing it from those that do not.

**Q: One of the classic discussions about Berkshire Hathaway is, "What will happen when Warren Buffett dies?" Although the**

traditional thinking has been that the share price will plummet, through online discussions I've been in touch with many people who have confidence that the effect will be small. Similarly, after the September 11 attacks, there was a lot of online editorial encouraging investors to hold on . . . So is the success of online financial sites going to reduce the extremes in market swings as those who would once have overreacted now get talked down by more moderate voices?

Some journalists have, on the other hand, consistently written about online chat and how this is used to hype people up about a given stock or the market, and have scapegoated Internet interactivity as one of the reasons for the steep market drop. We think both of these premises, that one and yours, can be true. The most important thing to take away from this is that the Internet is a powerful tool—how that tool is used is what's at issue. At Fool.com, we harness the Internet to educate, and by it we and many others have learned a tremendous amount about business, the stock market, the economy, and the importance of finance to achieving success in life. And yes, many of us probably do have a much more level head as a result—that's what comes of education. Then again, others will use the Internet to hype penny stocks.

Q: Before the recent crash I was on a trajectory to achieve my goals with a 7 percent per year return. Now, I have lost about 20 percent of my portfolio. Is it realistic to think that with astute planning now I might increase earnings enough to meet the original goals?

Well, first recognize that even making the statement you've made is excellent. Most Americans have no plan. So most have no idea that they were on track for a retirement with 7 percent annual returns, and many haven't quantified being down 20 percent (many don't have much at all, anyway). Thus, congratulations are in order that you've gone as far as you have already. We think it's probably best to keep your goals intact and to revise your time frame. You were basing your original premise on numbers generated by a hot stock market whose heat was unsustainable. A drop-off is a healthy and organic process, though always hard to take for psychologies that had adjusted themselves toward higher and higher expectations. The best thing you can do now is, yes, to plan astutely and work hard and keep investing, but also to ratchet down your own expectations so that, if anything, they would be exceeded! That will more likely lead to happiness.

**Q: What's the best way to quantify risk? Previously I have concentrated on return rather than risk, but after the last one and a half years, risk becomes much more important since I will have to start withdrawing retirement funds in four to five years.**

Let's roll up our sleeves and dig through some numbers, here, because you've asked a numbers question.

Risk is defined as *the quantifiable likelihood of loss or less than expected returns*. The key word there is "quantifiable." Because risk is a *relative* thing, where one investment is riskier than another, you need a baseline or benchmark level of risk that everyone is willing to agree upon.

In the United States, and around the world, U.S. Treasury securities (bills/bonds) are generally considered "risk-free." They are guaranteed by the full faith and credit of the United States of America, and as far as risk goes, that's about as good as it gets for most people. So, our benchmark is a U.S. Treasury, specifically the three-month Treasury bill. Whatever the three-month T-bill pays, at any point in time, is widely considered the risk-free rate. All other expected returns are measured against it. Any investment you make, by definition, is riskier than the three-month T-bill.

If you're investing in anything other than the three-month T-bill, you MUST expect a higher return on your money, otherwise why take the risk? The amount of extra return above and beyond the risk-free rate is called a risk premium. The size of the risk premium depends, of course, on how risky the investment is. For example, the three-month T-bill currently yields 2.09 percent. A three-month CD is yielding about 2.20

percent. Not a huge difference, but it illustrates the difference between two fairly similar investment vehicles over the same period of time. The CD, which is backed by the guv'ment's FDIC insurance, is only slightly more risky than the Treasury bill, and you need to expect a slightly higher return for the additional risk you're taking.

Now, without getting too complicated, one of the factors in determining expected return is time horizon. How long will my money be tied up? The longer your money is tied up, the more return you need to make. Example: The ten-year U.S. Treasury bond is yielding 4.59 percent, 2.5 percent higher than the three-month Treasury bill. You are being compensated for tying up your money for a longer period of time.

When you compare investments that span different time horizons, you have to compare apples to apples. If the ten-year U.S. Treasury is paying me 4.59 percent per year, a ten-year corporate bond needs to have a higher yield to justify taking the risk of buying a company's bonds. After all, we can buy the government bond and be virtually guaranteed 4.59 percent. The safest ten-year corporate bonds currently yield 5.12 percent. You can obviously see that you're being compensated for investing in a riskier security, relatively speaking. The risk premium is 0.53 percent annually.

And *that* is how you quantify risk. If you're asking how to quantify the risk of your investment in Disney or GE, let us say, you must come up with what you expect or need your return to be and then weigh that against the company's likelihood to achieve it. And then you might weigh that likelihood against the likelihoods of other companies beating that! Etc.

Do you see how this thinking can drive a person insane? We think it's right to be well aware of risk and the possibility of underperformance or loss, but not to overdo this.

Q: Where should I focus the extra dollars in my budget? Should I create the Ideal Me (particularly the steps that require a cash outlay) before anything else, or spread the wealth over a number of goals?

You're trying to account for several factors here. You don't want to throw off your long-term goals, but there is a reason they call it an *emergency* fund. The general rule is to direct 50 percent of your savings to your retirement accounts and 50 percent to your emergency fund until your emergency fund has reached the ideal size for you. Of course every rule has room for personalization. For example, if you feel uneasy about your job security, now is the time to supercharge your emergency fund and pull back from some of the longer-term goals. But building up that emergency fund should ultimately be your first priority.

**Q: Would it be best to liquidate my current stock holdings, and forgo a Roth IRA and three-month cash buffer to pay off my car loan completely right now (which is my only source of "bad debt" at present), or take a more balanced approach to pay down the debt as quickly as possible while maintaining my investments and savings?**

"Bad debt" in Motley Fool parlance is debt with double-digit interest rates. As a top priority, it is highly worth eliminating this, and our answer here is given under the context that *you* know yourself better than we do, and ultimately only *you* can decide what's best for your situation. Otherwise, here's our take: The emergency fund is critical, and a higher priority than paying off the car early. Your current stock holdings may be worth liquidating, but are they profitable (and therefore will generate a capital gain)? If so, we'd probably not sell those this year. If not, if they're underwater for you, you'll be generating a tax loss that may be useful to you this year, and that may carry forward if it's greater than $3,000—so you have a tax question there that must be considered apart from the car. It *is* worth, we think, delaying your Roth IRA investment in order to pay off a double-digit car loan. The stock market will get you 10 percent in an average year; if you're paying at least that and possibly more, get the debt out.

Q: How should medical insurance fit into my plans? How important is it both now and in the future?

Medical insurance is a prime consideration at any stage of life. We consider its cost an indispensable part of anyone's budget at *every* stage of life. That's particularly true for those who retire prior to age sixty-five, the age when Medicare becomes effective. Prior to that age, many early retirees have discovered such insurance is difficult to obtain. Indeed, the lack of or high cost of such insurance prior to Medicare age poses the largest obstacle to an early retirement.

Q: I have a universal policy that I began back in '86 for both my wife and me. I have not paid on it for several years, instead using the cash value to fund the insurance. Are these policies worth refunding after the cash value is gone? Is term insurance the only way to go?

Rarely should insurance be purchased as an investment. It should be used for the protection of income for your family in the event you check out early. In your case, the horse has already left the barn. Now you must decide whether the coverage provided by your policy is worth the cost of that coverage in comparison to what you may purchase elsewhere. Additionally, you must decide whether the investments within that policy compare favorably to investments available to you outside of it. Those comparisons are the only way you may make a reasoned decision whether to keep or junk the coverage you now have, and only you have all the facts necessary to make that determination.

Q: What exactly does a financial planner bring to the table— is it worth the charge?

It certainly can be. It depends on the following factors:

- How much money you have
- The complexity of your finances

- Your interest in doing the research
- The value of time, to you, that could be spent not studying money matters
- Your expertise in money matters
- Your level of confidence in your understanding

There are many reasons to seek the services of a paid financial advisor, ranging all the way from a helping hand in getting off to a solid start early in your life to, later in life, calling in a hired gun to help with a complex mess at a critical moment. Consider where you sit on this continuum and give it some thought.

When it comes to picking a planner, there is one key question to ask: Who's paying the planner? "Free" financial planning services scare us. Obviously, the planner is making a living somehow, right? We haven't met one yet who works as a volunteer to the middle class. So where's the money coming from? If it isn't coming from you, it's obviously coming from the insurance company, mutual fund company, annuity, or investment program that the planner is recommending. So who's he working for, you or them?

A fee-only financial planner works for *you*. You pay for his time and expertise and, presumably, he leads you safely through the financial minefields to the land of personal wealth. Of course finding a financial planner, especially if you don't have appreciable assets generally in excess of $100,000, can be tough and expensive. If you're interested in getting some personal advice, double-checking your plan, or just (like many of us) building your first plan, we of course recommend our TMF Money Advisor service. You can learn more about it at TMFMA.Fool.com.

# 11

# More Questions, More Answers

Man who waits for roast duck to fly into mouth must wait very, very long time.

— CHINESE PROVERB

We consistently receive excellent questions and comments at Fool.com—ranging from the rather simple to the deeply complex. And while we don't have a magic formula into which you can plug three variables to find all the money needed to pay down your debts or every necessary insight to find stock market winners, we *can* help you get started with your own research.

Please remember that your research work will pay out significant rewards to you and your family for decades and generations to come. We hope you'll find ways to share your financial learning with family members.

Okay, more questions as we finish out What to Do Now.

**Q: Why am I so insecure about making investment decisions?**

On some level, we all are. Consider what happened to Enron Corporation and its shareholders in 2001. Some of the

THE MOTLEY FOOL'S WHAT TO DO WITH YOUR MONEY NOW     141

world's brightest investors are sitting on losses of 100 percent today, in the wake of (as of this writing) possible executive fraud and certain mismanagement at the company, and possibly criminal negligence by its auditor. It's the sort of collapse that fosters a feeling of insecurity in all of us. But really, that suspicion and anxiety—that *insecurity*—can be healthy.

One of the great modern CEOs, Andrew Grove at Intel, co-wrote an outstanding business book entitled *Only the Paranoid Survive*. There's some truth to the title. The challenge is to use those feelings to intensify your commitment to learn: to read more, ask more questions, be less hasty and, ultimately, to be more deliberate in your actions. So how do you balance insecurity with determination?

We suggest gradually building a platform of confidence around a basic set of precepts you know to be true—simple yet profound notions. Start with the tenets of the Ideal You and these three investing basics:

1. The stock market has historically returned 11 percent per year on average.
2. Even were that rate of return to decline slightly, the stock market is likely to be the best place for your long-term savings this century.
3. The stock market's average return can be earned inexpensively through an index fund.

Upon that foundation, build your own library of financial knowledge as you go. Maybe you'll draw a shuffle of early conclusions such as the following:

1. I know very little about high-technology stocks and should avoid them.
2. If I'm going to buy a company, I must be able to explain its business in sixty seconds or less.
3. I should always review a company's financial statements before investing.
4. Between The Motley Fool discussion boards and my group of friends, family, and colleagues, I should and can

gather substantial amounts of information in advance of any investment I make.

Q: As a rookie investor I'm confused about the best place to start researching stocks. Is there a screening/forecasting tool that's relatively reliable and easy to use? I don't have a lot of extra time, but I want to educate myself before I take the plunge. How much time do I realistically need to spend to own stocks?

First, determine how much time you want, and can afford, to spend managing your money. If it's less than a few hours a year, you're better off indexing. Blend stock and bond index funds as you see fit. Take a total of two hours to research the different historical returns of different indices. Make your allocation decision. Direct regular investments into those index funds. Then reevaluate your assumptions and allocation for two hours at the end of each year. Voilà. That's your investment strategy defined in no more than two to four hours per year.

If, however, you have intellectual energy for investing and can dedicate anywhere from ten to 300 hours per year to individual stocks, then start adding stocks to your basic index portfolio. Always require that you can complete the following:

- Before you invest in a company, pull aside your spouse, significant other, or a close friend. Then in sixty seconds, explain to them what the company does and how it makes its money.

- Grab a pencil or computer keyboard and compose a short list of the primary reasons you're purchasing the stock. Complete the task by listing out your primary concerns about the investment.

- Make an estimate of the performance of the investment over your projected holding period. Let's say you decide to buy the New York Times Co. (NYSE: NYT) at $43 per share today. Further, let's say you hope to hold shares of the business for the next ten years. Then estimate what annual returns you expect—9 percent, 11.5 percent, 13 percent per year?

Once you've done the necessary research, these three tasks can take less than thirty minutes. Redo the three tasks when you feel your assumptions have changed.

Now, how about actually doing the stock research? First, we cannot recommend highly enough that you stick to investments that represent your life, your job, your home, your town, your interests, your pastimes, and your knowledge. If you are to beat the stock market's average return, you'll need to understand a company's products, its industry, its competition, its financials, and its executive team *better than most other people*. The first best research is just getting familiar with the organization.

From there, visit www.freeedgar.com or Yahoo! or our site and obtain the company's last year of financial statements. Here it's time to begin running financial ratios. For our approach to analyzing an individual company, please read these articles at Fool.com: Fool.com/school/howtovaluestocks.htm.

Q: When you analyze a stock, how do you know how big of a universe to use when comparing its performance to "everything else"? For example, if I'm considering a hardware maker (one of the areas hit hardest in the tech meltdown), do I compare it to only its largest competitors, or to hardware makers in general, or to the Nasdaq, or the S&P 500, or the Wilshire 5000? I've read that our benchmark is the S&P 500 performance. But is that always true?

Great question. We really do prefer using the S&P 500 or Wilshire 5000 as our benchmarks. Why? Because any one of us could easily obtain those general market returns. All it takes is a phone call to Vanguard or to your broker to purchase the stock version of the S&P index fund, Spiders (AMEX: SPY).* If you can get the market average with no more than five minutes of effort a year, any additional effort ought to be 1) geared toward beating the average, and thus 2) tracked back against that market average index.

None of this is to say you shouldn't track your hardware maker's performance against its lead competitors, its broader industry, and any other relevant groupings. Set it all up in a spreadsheet or in a portfolio tracker online. It can only serve to provide you more context. That said, we do think the ultimate comparison is back to the easily duplicated general market's return.

**Q: Many companies seem to "cook" their stated earnings, making it difficult to calculate a real P/E ratio. Does the average investor have to learn to dive into the depths of the company reports to ferret this out or can this information be obtained in other ways?**

The most frequently used yardstick for stock valuation is the price-to-earnings ratio, also known as the P/E ratio or the earnings multiple. The P/E ratios of various stocks are batted around a lot by investors. The P/E ratio is only a single valuation tool, but it's still useful. There's an easy way to calculate it. Simply divide a company's total market capitalization (price × total shares outstanding) by its total earnings for the past year. Let's consider the case of the fictional company, Philly Cheese Steak Inc. Here are the basic variables you'll need:

**Philly Cheese Steak Inc.**
- Share Price: $10
- Total Shares Outstanding: 25 million

---

* Haven't heard of "Spiders," by the way? The name is an acronym that stands for S&P Depositary Receipts, but all you really need to know here is that they function like an index fund, but exist as a stock. For those who want more information on Spiders, just type that word into our search engine at Fool.com. This gives us an opportunity to remind you that if you're looking for more definitions or financial concepts or the Motley Fool take on any of these things, use the search box on our main page at Fool.com to dig out more information.

- Total Market Capitalization: $10 × 25 million = $250 million
- Total Year's Earnings: $20 million
- P/E or Earnings Multiple: $250 million/$20 million = 12.5

Philly Cheese Steak Inc. is priced at $250 million and made $20 million in profit over the past year. That means that the company is trading at a price that is 12.5 times its earnings. Simple stuff. Its earnings multiple is 12.5.

The question is: Is that really a useful way to gauge a company's price? Our answer is *yes* and *no*.

On the affirmative side, it tells you what the market is paying for a dollar of the company's earnings. It gives a ballpark range for projected annual sales and earnings growth (in the 12.5 percent per year range). And it gives you a point of comparison with industry competitors and the market in general (historically, the S&P 500 has traded at an earnings multiple of 16).

On the negative side, as you rightly note, companies can "manage" their earnings. They can pollute reality by scoring, as earnings, deals for which they have not yet earned the cash. They can hide compensation costs by issuing dilutive stock options. Investors who rely exclusively on the earnings multiple overrate the accuracy of a company's earnings. This is why we also recommend that stock investors run analyses on the cash flow statement (for more on doing that, you can read our *Motley Fool Investment Guide* or check out our online seminar "Crack the Code: Read Financial Statements Like a Pro," available in our online store at Foolmart.com).

**Q: Some sources say that the average P/E today is much larger than at previous bear market bottoms. Does this mean we're in for a longer period before recovery?**

It may. There's no question now that over the past few years, the overall stock market was being priced (at an excess of 30 times earnings) for near-perfect corporate performance. Clearly, those heightened expectations have been leveled by the recession.

stion you're asking is whether the recovery will
given present valuations off present and projected
l Miller, the outstanding fund manager at Legg
...on, has said that he expects earnings to rebound with relative ease. However, he adds, present valuation off these re-
duced earnings is still high enough that there won't be any
roaring comeback on the stock market.

In other words, he appears to agree with the theme of your
question.

All of that said, we do believe a recovery lies ahead in the
oncoming years. It may not bring 15 percent annual growth. It
may not even bring 10 percent annual growth. But if it brings
anywhere north of 7 percent annual growth over the next five
years, then we still believe a total market index fund is a brain-
less way to get very competitive rates of return.

Q: Are there corresponding indices in Canada, Germany, or
internationally that are comparable to the Standard and Poor's
500 Index in America? And since there are a number of indices,
should I be diversified into the S&P 500 Index, a small-cap
index, and a total bond index simultaneously, or is investing
strictly in the S&P 500 acceptable? Mostly I wonder about how
much diversification a person needs, and how best to achieve it
when using index funds.

There are a few foreign indices you might want to take a look
at. In our Index Center at Fool.com, we look specifically at the:

- FTSE 100—The British equivalent of the Dow Jones In-
  dustrial Average.
- Hang Seng—The measurement of the Hong Kong stock
  market.
- Nikkei 225—The most widely watched stock average in
  Japan.

Another index you may want to consider is the MSCI
EAFE—The Morgan Stanley Capital International EAFE (Europe, Australia, and the Far East) Index—which was created in

1969 to measure the investment returns of developed countries outside of North America.

We do think the Vanguard Total Stock Market Index Fund in America suffices for the majority of investors looking to reduce the fees and taxes of professional money management while earning the stable, long-term return from stocks. That said, there are certainly cases to be made for buying more than one index.

The advantage of adding a small-cap or mid-cap index is that, historically, the universe of smaller companies has tended to outgrow that of larger companies. International indexing can provide you with some additional diversification . . . though the real opportunity would appear to lie in indexing politically stable, emerging economies. Finally, adding non-stock indices layers your portfolio with different levels of risk and rates of return. This can be particularly important, as we've noted, for investors who will need to withdraw money in less than five years.

Finally, to be clear, there is no evidence that, after a few decades, investors would end up with more money if they diversified beyond the S&P 500. But if you want possible protection from market volatility and want to take a shot at beating the overall market's average returns, then adding some smaller, specialized indices isn't a bad idea. For beginners though, we suggest sticking with one or two of the broad-based ones.

Q: When people suggest certain percentages for allocating one's investments (e.g., stocks, bonds, cash), does one generally include *all* of one's assets? For example, in our retirement savings, currently about 75 percent of our money is invested in stock funds. But that means that only 44 percent of our *total* assets—not counting equity in our house or our life insurance policies—are invested in equities.

Yes, when evaluating your overall financial plan, you should include *all* of your assets. This will give you the full picture you need.

You should also consider your liabilities. If you have thousands of dollars in credit card debt, don't ignore that as you apportion your assets between stocks, bonds, and funds. Many people actually have the money to pay off their double-digit interest-rate debt, but they don't do so, because they're not looking at their total financial picture and plan.

**Q: I already have a few stocks in my portfolio, and I'm now going to allocate a certain amount of money from each paycheck to purchase more stock. My question is, how do I select which stock to add money to? Are there any guidelines to follow, or do I just jump in, do my best, and see what happens?**

First of all, it's great that you're regularly adding savings to your investment portfolio. Since you've decided to add money to stocks you already own, start by ranking your present investments from "most attractive" to "least attractive." In those classifications, include a variety of factors. Which business do you believe in the most? Which business is priced inexpensively relative to its projected future growth? Which business do you know best?

The ranking system will guide your investment decisions. Write out some assumptions on your purchases so that you can evaluate how effective your ranking criteria were when you look back at them months and years from now. And once you have this ranking list, take a look at your overall portfolio allocation.

Four back-of-the-envelope suggestions we can make:

1. Do not own more than twenty stocks. It's extremely difficult to track them all and unlikely with that number that you'll beat the performance of a total market index fund. Our recommendation is six to twelve holdings.

2. Do not add money to any position that represents more than 15 percent of your total portfolio. However, we're not inclined to sell down holdings that, through their excellence, have grown to very large positions in our portfolio.

3. Look closely at the bottom of your ranking list. Are you sure you want to continue holding the bottom one or two stocks? Do you really believe in them?

4. Remember to track your performance against a total market index fund. It's possible you should be opening an index fund position and adding more money to that over time.

Finally, please note that your question involves some deeper investment thinking outside the purview of this book, which is primarily focused on What to Do Now as regards investing and money decisions toward the end of a bear market. Please take a look instead at our investment trilogy from Simon & Schuster, which begins with *You Have More Than You Think,* our starter money guide designed to help you make your first investment; then proceeds to *The Motley Fool Investment Guide,* which gives our primary thinking about stock market investing and starting and managing your own portfolio; and then concludes with *Rule Breakers, Rule Makers,* with our most advanced and aggressive personal approaches to investing.

*Read!*

Q: How do you reconcile the following? We hear the popular advice to diversify stock holdings across ten or twenty companies, in order to reduce risk. But we also have limited time to "really understand" individual companies we own. Realistically, I might be able to only follow three to five businesses (alongside my full-time life!).

Great question. Simple answer. Let's say you have $100,000 to invest for five years or more. Normally, we'd recommend, say, eight holdings of $12,500 each. Know those companies thoroughly. Follow their quarterly earnings. Be sure to have some larger companies there for ballast.

Aha, wait! You say you can only find the time to invest in three companies. Hey, that's great. Consider taking the $100,000 out and splitting it this way: $10,000 each in three separate companies; $50,000 into a total market index fund;

and $20,000 into a mid-cap index fund. The index funds you won't have to follow but once every few years. Truly. But the stocks you'll have to follow much more closely.

As you add new savings, add it to the positions you feel most comfortable with (per the ranking list above). It may be that you can save another $100,000 over the next fifteen years and decide to invest all of it into index funds.

## Conclusion

This brings us to the close of questions, and the close of this central section of the book.

Of course, all of us continue to have questions about the management of our money. There is no end, dear Fool, to these questions. We hope there is no end to your curiosity, either. Therefore, we close this Q&A section of the book with a reading list. These are page-turning financial books from which we think many can enjoyably learn a great deal.

- *Buffett: The Making of an American Capitalist,* by Roger Lowenstein
- *One Up on Wall Street,* by Peter Lynch
- *Famous Financial Fiascos,* by John Train
- *The Death of the Banker,* by Ron Chernow
- *John Bogle on Investing: The First 50 Years,* by John Bogle
- *Common Stocks and Uncommon Profits,* by Philip Fisher

We're confident you'll appreciate any and all of these, and will learn important lessons along the way.

The way forward.

Forward, to "What Next?"

# INTERLUDE

**Before** bidding adieu to the past and the present, let us note again that the last five years have actually been pretty good, particularly when you consider what poor years 2000 and 2001 were. The S&P 500 index, for the five years from 1997 through 2001, rose an annualized 9.2 percent (not including dividends)—below historical norms by just a percentage point. Add in the great two years preceding, and the annualized return on the S&P 500 for the past seven years has been a whopping 14.0 percent (again, not including dividends).

Which is why even the lessons we have learned over the past twenty-four months must be put into context. We're not going to overreact to a few bad years, and neither should you. While we have resolved to focus more tightly on profitable business models in our investing, for instance, that doesn't mean we're "never ever" going to invest in a company that has yet to show profits. Part of the legacy of the past seven years has shown that to be quite a successful way to invest, when done prudently. True to our 1999 book on the subject, we continue to search for Rule Breakers, right alongside Rule Makers.

That 9.2 percent return, by the way, means that the most recently completed five-year period once again provides yet another in which you're better off sitting in stocks than in certificates of deposit (CDs). When you look at the history of the stock market from 1901 to 1906, 1902 to 1907, 1903 to 1908, and forward like that, in over 90 percent of those five-year increments the stock market beats CDs.

All of this is just to point out that if you were Rip Van Winkle, fell asleep five years ago and missed all the glory and the pain, and woke up today, you'd say, "Okay. That's an acceptable rate of return." Before napping again. And we think if you did fall asleep today and wake up five years from now, odds on you'll wake up and deliver the exact same line. So, in a world in which too often we look back, it's time to look forward. To ask, "What next?" To escape the "Rowboat Syndrome," as Vanguard founder Jack Bogle has called it.

Don't know the Rowboat Syndrome? Well, when you paddle a rowboat, you're going forward but looking back. It's the way too many of us proceed through life and make decisions; we overweight our most recent experience, and project that experience immediately into the future. It's the reason so many people buy high and then sell low, both of them individual mistakes that, compounded, are deadly. Many who were unknowledgeable about the stock market and therefore afraid of its risks waited a long time to invest. In many cases, they had to move out of debt toward savings in the first place. Finally, after having watched business and stock market success endure for three, four, five consecutive years—*looking backward*—they say, "I can't believe how much I've missed and how well I would've done. I can't stay outta this forever. I'm in!" Rowing their boat, they buy at a time when the market is likely due for some downtime. So then after that next succeeding twelve or eighteen months in which the market does poorly, they're sick of losing money. They're still rowing that boat along, going, "Gosh, things have been bad, things really *are* bad—I've got to get out of this." So, they end up selling just as the market is probably due for some uptime. They've made the very same mistake on both the front end and the back end: looking backward to base their decisions about the future.

Thus, before we consider together "What next?" we ask you not to be pursued or haunted by the Rowboat Syndrome. In order to go forward, you want to be looking forward.

# PART THREE

# WHAT
# NEXT?

Whether you've had business success or business failure over the last few years, or whether you've had investment success or investment failure, doesn't matter much right now. These have become the stuff of history. What actually matters is what happens next. Hence the section title. (Ingenious, no?)

When we talk about "What next?" we need to clear up any misconceptions up front. We are *not* tea leaf readers. We do *not* believe in astrology in any way, shape, or form. And we know the regrettable records of analysts, economists, and every other carcass of a pundit when it comes to predicting market or business future. Predictions may make good headline copy for journalists, but that's about all they're good for. You rarely ever see these journalists follow up a year later to show the actual performance of their brilliant "experts" (an overused word in our society). Why? Because then they wouldn't be considered experts anymore. And journalists wouldn't know where to go for good headline copy!

When we speak of "What next?" you will find few predictions in this closing section. As change is the most dependable earthly constant, it only takes one significant change (whether it's the fall of communist governments in 1989, the sudden mass adoption of the Internet beginning in 1995, or September 11) to start a new trend. That trend then gives rise to other changes leading to other new trends. By that time, we wind up so far removed from our original thinking as to render most typical predictions not just "wrong," but completely irrelevant. They have nothing whatsoever to say to what has actually subsequently happened.

When *we* speak, therefore, of "What next?" we believe not so much in trying to predict a future as we believe in *creating* or *ensuring* that future through good thinking, planning, and doing. "What next" is not an invitation or license to prognosticate; it is a collective nudge to join in the craft, to contribute to the forming and execution of the blueprint.

Shall we?

# 12

# Make
# Life
# Convenient

In this closing section, like the opening one, each of our points speaks both to business and to investing. The two go together, especially for those of us who fancy ourselves "business-focused investors" (a term we find more useful than many of the old frameworks of thinking, like the obfuscating clichés of "value investors" versus "growth investors"). Business-focused investors try not to look too much at the zigs and zags. And they certainly don't use chart patterns to make investment decisions. Some people seem to live and die by those patterns, but like living and dying by tobacco, we'd prefer just to skip the stuff altogether.

Our first resolution as we proceed into the future is to *make life convenient*.

## THE BUSINESS LESSON

We return to Steven Cristol, the consultant turned songwriter turned *Simplicity Marketing* author, who points to some obvious signs of information overload and overcomplication in our society. Crest now comes in something like thirty-seven different varieties when you add up all the containers (tube, pump, etc.), flavors, and promises ("tartar control," etc.). It's increasingly difficult just to buy TOOTHPASTE anymore at your supermarket. You have to scan the aisle carefully and sort through all the options. And this is just one consumer product. When you consider the oodles of choices you have in product types, colors, shapes, sizes, tastes, promises, names, model numbers, etc. etc. etc. as a consumer going through our society today, you may well conclude with Cristol that we live in an age of "overchoice." Within this labyrinth of choices, all the information you need to digest, and the demands on your time, you come to yearn for Simplicity (with a capital S). And more to the point within this section, the businesses that offer simplicity will in our view come to dominate those that do not.

Because most of us just don't have TIME to make all these choices.

Cristol said to us, at our company meeting, "Who here has been to the W Hotel? Okay, if you've been to one of these up-scale chain hotels, you know that they have this button on the phone in your room called 'Whatever, Whenever.' I find myself using this button all the time in every circumstance, which I guess is the point of the button." Right. Simplicity. Cristol pointed to the feature-crawl going on in hotel phones, where many of them now have an elaborate dashboard of individual buttons surrounding the traditional numbers, buttons that ostensibly cater to your every whim: "Concierge," "Room Service," "Laundry," "Front Desk," "Wake-up," etc. It's not always clear how one is intended to use some of these buttons, based on their ambiguous labels. But even if they were labeled perfectly, many of us would still be frustrated in using them just because of the time it takes to win out within the battlefield of choices.

Cristol then went on with the key observation: "It occurred to me that the 'Whatever, Whenever' button is just the zero button for operator that we all were used to using in hotels before they got all these new phones! You'd hit zero and get the operator and then ask for whatever you wanted and get directed that way by the operator." The W Hotel, in other words, is just relabeling, rebranding (with two words that start with W, unsurprisingly), the 0 operator button! This is the state of our society in many ways, that businesses have to work at seeing things differently in order to retrieve simplicity from its skulking dark spot in the corner. Simplicity—here synonymous with convenience—is something businesses must truly work at by seeing things from their customers' viewpoint, and only a handful of businesses truly get this.

Contrast this with our recent local experiences at a Best Buy during the Christmas shopping season. This retailer of electronics laid out all its digital camera models on the shelves, locked to the shelf to prevent stealing. If you wished either to purchase a model or to inquire about one, you were asked to wait in line for a sales guy. You waited twenty minutes for this privilege (especially frustrating as you already knew the one you want, had researched it on the Internet, you didn't need any sales advice), and as you finally got to the front of the line you said you'd like this brand and model. "We don't have any of those in stock," says the sales guy. "We're out. Of the models out on the shelves," of which there are thirty-five to forty, "we only have this and this and this and this other one."

Now maybe it makes good business sense among the strategists at Best Buy HQ to keep your customers in the store by showing them the goods they're interested in, even when you don't have them. We don't claim to know this business really well; maybe that increases foot traffic and time spent in the store, and those are the metrics you're watching. But Best Buy lost a customer forever that day, simply because either store policy or staffer oversight failed to indicate with stickers or labels that of the thirty-five brands on display, thirty of them couldn't be purchased for Christmas presents from their store or "any other in the D.C. area." Making it hard to be your customer will redound back upon your business in time. Those happy guys on the Best Buy television commercials we're watching sure look different from our friends in line that day.

Good businesses make life convenient. Check that: *Great* businesses make life convenient, as the number of those that achieve convenience for their customers are so few as to merit a prouder adjective.

Does the company *you* work for make life convenient for its customers? Do you see ways to help your customers cut extra corners, or dispense with paperwork, confusion, or long lines?

Do you, as a customer of businesses yourself, remember any moments when a business achieved this for you? Do you remember how you felt? Haven't you become their lifetime customer? Chances are if this has happened to you you've told your friends—probably many friends. As lowly consumers we feel uplifted and honored by any businesses that conveniently extend convenience to us, as their customers. More business people should remember this when they take off their own lowly consumer hats and prepare to plan for their business approach.

Because let's be square about this: Perhaps the defining personality trait of the mass-market American consumer is *laziness*. If you look out across our fair shores and the 3,000-mile expanse in between, you'll find clear indications that 300 million or so of your countrymen want more and more stuff delivered. At first, years and years ago, it was just their mail. Then it was pizza. Then it was lots of other food besides. Then it was the trinkets of e-commerce: books, CDs, videos, etc. And wherever possible many of us have since made some portion of our homes our offices—we wanted our work delivered, so to speak. What's next? Mail-order baby delivery followed by mail-order education leading to mail-order diplomas? From a parental standpoint, those sound convenient.

Plus, we're willing to pay up for convenience. The $30 tab being charged for breakfast room service at a Virginia hotel one weekend—a breakfast consisting of a pot of coffee and a basket of Danish for two—reminds us how many dollars we will part with in order to have someone else do the work for us. Even when it isn't that much work. (And how about the gall of those establishments that add a 17 percent gratuity automatically on the receipt you sign, and right below this "service charge" is also a separate blank line for a "Tip"!)

Convenience feeds laziness. In fact, we're generally quite

willing to compromise on quality in order to get our convenience. How many great brands illustrate this point? From Gap (which certainly doesn't make the best leisurewear) to Microsoft (which doesn't make the best software), to AOL (which doesn't offer the best Internet), to Starbucks (which doesn't make the best coffee—well, at least it can't truly be worth $5 for every few ounces—didn't some coffee industry study come out and report that the average American can make a cup of coffee for 8 cents?). So, the $2.50 or $25 or $250 that we are often willing to pay for convenience is very valuable! And now you see why we think it behooves you to work for and invest in companies that earn such value by dint of their focus on convenience.

Again, Microsoft has succeeded in making software convenient by trying to work everything onto a single platform that we can all adopt and use. Programmers don't like it, and competitors don't like it, but where's the seismic consumer complaint about Microsoft? Where are the barbarians at the gate, the angry, teeming masses? Nowhere. The Department of Justice case was agitated by industry insiders who got the ear of government. Most of the rest of us couldn't care less.

From the get-go, America Online has made it convenient for tens of millions worldwide to sign up online. The AOL main screen has hardly changed over the past decade, while the value of the company has increased by billions. By contrast, consider other Web sites out there and other technology companies who are constantly thinking they need some great new offering. Things need to look better. They need to look different. "We don't have it quite right." Meantime, AOL has said they've evaluated their business model and most people just want e-mail and maybe to send instant messages. The optimal mass-market use of the online medium is simply as a basic communication tool. So, they hardly ever change. And in so doing, they've kept their customer experience simple and uncomplicated (once you found out how to disable those annoying pop-ups), striking a blow for Simplicity and adding a few tens of billions to their market cap. They've crossed the

chasm in terms of getting mainstream America involved in
their business, and they've done it by focusing not on change,
not on better prices, but on actually making life convenient for
the people using their service.


## THE INVESTING LESSON

The investment yang to the business yin on this point is simply that as investors we should be making our lives convenient, as convenient as possible. Just as successful businesses
do for their customers, so we can do and should do for ourselves and for our families.

For us, investing was made very convenient because our
dad taught us from very early on about the stock market and
about business. That's been an active ongoing conversation
running since our youth. And there are age-appropriate lessons that parents can teach at each point. For us, about the
time that we reached Wiffle ball age, Dad sat us down with
*Value Line,* the thick and imposing black book full of business
and investment statistics for thousands of corporations. Dad
brought that book to life by teaching us about net profit mar-
gin and about return on equity and other things that you need
to know as an investor. Then, when we turned eighteen, he
gave us each the investment portfolios that he'd started at our
birth. A wonderful thing, something we're extremely grateful
for, something that ultimately made The Motley Fool possible
because rather than taking jobs at someone else's company, in
our mid-twenties we were able to take a risk and start something ourselves.

Our dad made this easy. He made our investing lives convenient. We've told this story a few thousand times but once
more can't hurt. He started us in the grocery store: "Hey kids!
Look! Chocolate pudding! We own some of the company that
makes it. Let's go get *more chocolate pudding!*" Which made
him a very popular dad. He was connecting the products and
services we liked with the completely novel idea that through
the stock market we could actually be part owners (however

small) of the manufacturer. It's a very, very basic lesson, but please ask yourself how many people out there really know that. How many people understand the stock market to be that, like a marketplace, like a farmer's market but rather than buying fruit you're buying pieces of companies, becoming an owner in a culture that celebrates ownership? Tocqueville admired America as a nation of owners, a people who value personal ownership. How many people really think of the stock market that way—as opposed to the great big gambling machine conceived earlier in the book by the Harley-Davidson guy, largely because he'd never received any education on the topic?

At The Motley Fool our mission is to educate, to amuse, and to enrich—which begins appropriately enough with education. We're glad we got an education, and if you are a teen or know a teen who lacks this education, get your hands on our new investment guide for teens—just out this year—because if young people truly understood these lessons of saving and making prudent spending and investment decisions, we would become such a stronger country.

Please note that convenience is double-edged. In making your life convenient as an investor—in studying more, saving more, starting earlier, trading less, paying fewer fees, paying less in taxes—you can sometimes allow convenience to be used as a kind of weapon against you if you aren't savvy to it. We're thinking here in particular about mutual funds. Mutual funds are indeed convenient, a wonderful convenience in that a single investment into a mutual fund gets you diversified into dozens of companies that would have been too costly and too much a bother to buy on your own. And certainly mutual funds are marketed very effectively for their convenience.

As you now know, the well-documented problem is that most mutual funds underperform the one mutual fund we like—the index fund—and do so dramatically over time. At a 10 percent rate of return, your $50,000 will compound over forty years to be worth $2.3 million. At a return rate of 8.5 percent—representing the annual 1.5 percent by which so many mutual funds underperform the index fund—your $50,000 will be worth just $1.3 million. Just a percent and a half, but worth $1 million less over that time span.

We have written earlier about the benefits of investing in index funds, and if you're looking for more on the topic just visit our online service at Fool.com or pick up *You Have More Than You Think,* our starter guide to thinking about money. The index fund simply buys hundreds or thousands of companies, passively, effectively giving you the whole market's average return for a comparatively tiny fee. With it you will outperform the vast majority of all other mutual funds year in and year out, and over time you'll be the person much more likely to have $2.3 million rather than $1.3 million. Does that sound like the right kind of convenience? You better believe it. But most ads coming from the fund industry don't come from index funds—which, if they advertised, would wind up costing you higher fees and making you less money. So the ads you see instead advertise the *convenience* and *comfort* and *ease* of investing in one or another underperforming mutual fund.

Yes, the index fund should be one's first and, for many, their last step when it comes to investing. As we've stated numerous times before, *any* effort you make toward investing in stocks should be with the intention of beating the market, of beating the index fund—otherwise, why bother? You can get the index fund's return quickly, easily, with no hassle.

We used another April Fool's joke to teach the lesson of the index fund, to encourage others to ask why $2 trillion is invested in professionally managed mutual funds that charge 1.5 percent per year to do worse than the average stock market return. Why is so much money invested there when you can call up Vanguard and get the return of the market at 0.2 percent per year instead of 1.5 percent per year?

So like our eMeringue gag, one year earlier, on April 1, 1998, we had filled up our main screen with a big announcement: an open letter of apology to our community. We're very, very sorry, we wrote. We at The Motley Fool have been telling you for the past four years that we don't think professionally managed mutual funds are really a good alternative for investors. We think just getting the index fund makes the most sense and we based that opinion on our back-tested mutual fund performance data, which we had typed into a spreadsheet. When we hit "print" to get the graph of the spreadsheet, we got a graph that suggested that 90 percent of mutual funds over the last ten years have done worse than average. But, unfortunately today we're here to apologize to you because it now looks like we printed the graph upside-down. Sure enough, it now turns out that 90 percent of mutual funds have in fact beaten the market's average return. We went on to say that we hoped that our mistake had *in no way* affected anyone's investment decisions. Here was the graph:

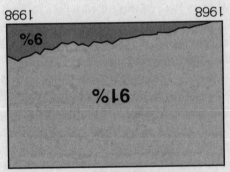

Comparison of Mutual Funds to
S&P 500

As you can see, the "incorrect" graph which we'd been using for five years was simply the "correct" graph flipped on its head, with all the lettering on the axes upside-down. Somehow, we'd been looking at that graph for five years and had not realized it was upside-down!

Now, we didn't think anyone would fall for our joke. But just for the fun of it, as the clock struck midnight on April 1, we linked in our e-mailbox to the announcement and invited people to respond to us directly. Over the next twenty-four hours we received a few thousand e-mails from people across the country. It's fair to say that two out of three knew we were joking: They saw the upside-down graph; they figured out it was April 1. But the one out of three who didn't get it means we got about 800 e-mails that for history's sake we've filed away because they're precious to us. Included in that group are more than one note from law firms letting us know they were already organizing a class action suit against The Motley Fool. One wonders how these firms' lawyers are allocating their *own* 401(k) decisions!

But we really got a treat when a fellow Fool in North Carolina e-mailed us saying we had to go and pick up a copy of the *Raleigh-Durham News & Observer*. Again, this is 8:00 A.M. the morning of April 1; we had only just put up our joke at midnight and now we're being told to go look at the Raleigh, North Carolina, paper eight hours later. Anyway, it turns out that just past midnight an employee in the Business Section at the paper had some space to fill. So, he simply went in and took large portions of our prank letter (also out as a press release) and pasted this to the front page of their Business Section. The headline read: "The Motley Fool Apologizes: 92% of All Mutual Funds Beat the Market."

We got an e-mail about six hours later from the executive editor of the business section. Paraphrased, he wrote, "Guys, your syndicated newspaper column is all across the country. Congratulations. I want you to know that I started working here three months ago and I was intending to pick up your column in short order, as well. I actually have the contract right on my desk. Anyway, I'm letting you know I am tearing up that contract. We will not be carrying The Motley Fool column in our newspaper. I plan to work here for the next thirty years, so if you'd like to reapply to have your column in our paper, drop the department a note sometime in the year 2029." So, we dropped him a note back and said we totally understood. We were hoping to teach a lesson with our joke but we understood how, given the way things played out, this would all have rubbed him the wrong way. Please understand, though, that while they wouldn't be carrying our column, we would include the story of the *Raleigh-Durham News & Observer* on April 1 in a future Motley Fool book. Voilà!

The index fund really does epitomize our lesson of making life convenient for yourself as an investor with the *best* form of convenience.

# 13

# Get
# Great People
# Involved

Behind the product lines, the financial statements, the strategic directions, and the stock market returns lie the *people* who make these happen. A bad mistake to make in both business and investing is to forget that this is true: to disconnect product creation from those who created it, to fail to reward the young woman who forced a strategic change, to fail to recognize the old man who watches your costs. Businesses never run themselves, despite how effortless some great businesses look. People run them. And good stock market returns are proof positive of the *people* at the business you're invested in. They're your sometimes heroes, your pedestrian Supermen.

So it is as true of your business and investing as it is of life: Your friends and acquaintances will rub off on you, helping make you what you are, and what you will become. So pick your friends carefully.

## THE BUSINESS LESSON

No corporate manager in recent times has so distinguished himself as a people person, a modern-day corporate humanist, as retired General Electric CEO Jack Welch. And the astonishing performance of GE stock over Welch's reign is proof positive of his approach and his genius. In his 2001 book *Jack: Straight from the Gut,* Welch points to something that Jim Collins talks about in his own excellent book, *Built to Last* (a study of companies that have achieved lasting success). It is that—perhaps from our education and our academic background—sometimes we *overrate* dissent.

Having learned something of this in our own business, we hold up Welch's and Collins's point as worthy of your consideration. So which is more important, to hear at the top levels of your company a variety of voices and have a lively ongoing debate about your operations and strategic direction, *or* to have alignment? The answer is of course something in the middle, but if you had to tip it one direction, we suggest you tip it toward alignment. Find a mission. Fix on your objectives. Arrive at your core values, the truths and personality traits you hold dear as a business. And then as early on and as frequently as possible, *actively exclude those people who don't share those values.* This is quite a contrary point in an age emphasizing diversity, multiculturalism, and different perspectives. We understand and appreciate those things; we can't help it; one of us went to Brown University. At the same time, these things taken to their logical conclusions make it very difficult to get stuff done. No surprise perhaps that these ideals flourish at universities, whose missions are to confer intellectual curiosity and to teach investigation, *not* explicitly to get stuff done: hit deadlines, negotiate with partners, please customers, beat competition, reward outside investors. We don't mean to overgeneralize, because of course there are homework deadlines and certainly competition in various forms on campus. But these are individual in nature compared to the challenge of trying to get a hundred, or a thousand, or a hundred thousand people to cooperate toward a profitable corporate end. No surprise that, of all constituents in higher education, business schools emphasize and indeed require (and grade) teamwork. That's exactly the right focus in business, in life outside the university. Which is why alignment counts for so very much.

So you got this? Get rid of people who don't align with your company's or team's vision and approach to fulfilling that vision. These dismissed employees will find other organizations to work at that meet their own values and needs. We read these days that only 50 percent of marriages work out. Well, we think the percentage would be very much lower when you're talking about an individual's true long-term fit with a given business. That's because we often spend months and hopefully years "researching" and getting to know a prospective spouse, but often only weeks or even just days getting to know our prospective employer. Prospective employers need to recognize that, as well.

In fact, author Jim Collins is a living, breathing example of what we're talking about here. In *Built to Last* he mentions that he had formerly worked for Hewlett-Packard, but says he could not abide one of their core values—it didn't represent who he was. He struggled with it for a long time and finally concluded that he would be better off, and Hewlett-Packard would be better off, if he found somewhere else to work. If individuals and companies alike shared more of this self-knowledge, employment turnover would involve less heartache and more shared happiness and productivity.

Jack Welch tells a story in his book about firing a substantial number of officers at General Electric in shocking fashion. He first of all sat with his managers and encouraged them to define a few core groups among staff. The first group were to be people who shared GE values and executed well. The second group were those who didn't share their values and also didn't execute. So far so good: Just about every business in the world can make smart decisions about these two groups, retaining the former, dismissing the latter. The real difficulty for business comes when evaluating the two additional groups: those who share your values but aren't executing, and those who don't share your values but really *do* execute.

Welch goes on to say that the problem has occupied him throughout his career and he has decided that if you share company values, then you'll get two or three chances to find your spot in the organization. If you share his values, you should be able to find success in the organization (especially since one of GE's values is being successful and winning). "But, in my forty-one years at General Electric," he goes on to say, paraphrased: I have come to the conclusion that the people that don't share your values, but still succeed, are a real problem in your business. On the one hand, the numbers look great. On the other, they often give rise to a fiefdom deviating from your values that can cause serious operational and structural problems over long periods of time.

So in this last group Jack Welch identified several top officers. At a meeting with his own higher-ups at GE at the time he said, to paraphrase, "I have some surprising and perhaps for some of you disturbing news. I am dismissing five leaders of the company. One of them is not executing. The other four don't share the values of General Electric. It's not that they lack integrity or ability. It's just that they don't share the core values of our mission. I asked them about it and they agree and so we are moving forward."

We think this is a really great story and perhaps you have encountered something similar in your own organization, or wish you'd had a manager this strong and good who would've enacted something similar. For a company to operate successfully and dependably over time, it must have alignment. We haven't always succeeded at that at The Motley Fool. In fact, come to think of it, each brother presently feels that the other should probably step down and find some other prima donna parade to strut around in.

Our differences aside, the Aristotelian in us begs to jump in at this point and recall again the Golden Mean. Surely, alignment itself is not a perfect ideal, a be-all, end-all. And we don't mean to suggest that. Our primary point in this chapter is about finding great people, not about obtaining perfect alignment in all cases. We just think most organizations don't value and nurture alignment enough. At the same time, we also need to strike some healthy balance between alignment and dissent.

In our experience, dissent is best fomented by inviting in outside advisors or putting outside directors on your company's board. This creates an arm's-length form of dissent out-side of your operations that you can use as a natural check on your own plans and actions.

In our first year of operations back in the early 1990s, one of the first things we did as a small team was to call in a few of our parents as an advisory group. One had been an execu-tive at Sara Lee. Another was running an advertising business in Chicago, while another was a longtime investor and econ-omist. Their advice was invaluable to us. They still don't know it because we didn't compensate them at all (shhhhhh!). But they emphasized really thinking through what it was we were trying to achieve. Why were we starting an organization? Did we want to go public? Was that the aim of the business? What were the values and where were we headed?

So now we've talked about great outside advisors, great managers, and great employees who create serious share-holder value, particularly when they're given incentives as di-rect owners of the business themselves. The topic is great people. And the surest way to find them is to search for peo-ple who are smarter than you are. In your own business it might be difficult. But so worth it.

The people that we pick, and the people that we exclude, these say a tremendous amount about who we are and what our businesses stand for.


## THE INVESTING LESSON

Like so many great business lessons, this one transfers seam-lessly into your investing. You are looking for good managers of your companies, good people with integrity and insight, stick-to-it-iveness, gusto, humility. Most of the great human virtues that we celebrate in our art and literature and history and culture are the very same that create business success. Forced to select between two managers, one of whom was a newbie possessed of outstanding character and the other of whom had experienced past success at a similar business, we would choose the former.

Of course, surrounding yourself with great people as an investor means more than just locating corporate managers. It's even more important whenever you select someone to proffer you advice about your money. Very few of us are qualified to make expert decisions across every one of the personal finance and investment categories that we have to do over the course of our life, so we need to find good help. For instance, David wishes that he'd had more help when he purchased his first car; he bought at the sticker price! (Our parents were good with investing, but didn't provide much personal finance guidance.) Truly, he didn't negotiate because he didn't realize as he walked into the car dealership that you could negotiate your car price down. So with what might have been his very first major purchase decision, he'd struck out.

When you consider all the decisions that we must make as adults—paying off debt, buying a house, taking out a mortgage, paying taxes, crafting a financial plan, buying insurance, drafting a will, making investments, setting up kids' accounts, paying for college, etc.—it quickly becomes obvious that no single adult is a true "expert" in all of these categories and so, yes, we absolutely do need advisors. With so many important decisions to make, you'd better *get great people involved!*

As we said earlier, and as you'll expect us to emphasize here again, make sure you know how these great people get paid. Don't be afraid to ask anybody who is giving you advice, "How do you get paid?" And, "How do you get paid more than that?" In other words, what is their incentive? A clear understanding up front of your advisor's own business model and incentives would have avoided so many errors worth billions of dollars for so many Americans. How many times at our book signings nationwide have we shaken hands with someone who's said, "I am here because I just got screwed. The person wasn't even unethical. He was just incompetent. But I didn't know enough to really surround myself with great people because back then I didn't even know the right questions to ask." Given that no standardized curriculum for money is taught in our schools at any level, it's not surprising, is it? We've loosed a whole bunch of adults on the world and have asked them to make lonely and often uninformed decisions across thirty-seven different categories of personal finance and investing. It's some kind of crazy. For this reason again, surround yourself with great people.

It must be noted, as the *Los Angeles Times* reported late last year, that most Americans with less than $100,000 will not even get a callback from most fee-only financial planners (our favorite kind, due to their objectivity). These planners want to work with higher-net-worth clients from whom they can obtain commensurately higher fees. Consequently, middle America has been saddled with few to no choices that provide convenient and affordable and truly objective advice, neither commission-driven nor (crucially) *fee-driven,* either.

Given that you are reading a Motley Fool book and given that last year The Motley Fool revolutionized independent financial advice by launching our TMF Money Advisor service mentioned earlier, we can't not point it out one last time. For less than $149 a year (a fraction of what a few hours with a good advisor would cost—see for yourself), you get truly independent, non-self-interested advice across any one of these thirty-seven different categories, year in and year out, from people who are *not* looking to "capture your assets" and charge you fees. Your questions are answered for you over the phone by experienced professionals through our partnership with The Ayco Company, L.P., a spin-off from American Express that had previously only provided its service to Fortune 500 executives. TMF Money Advisor has thus brought this service to the mass-consumer market, a market that has neither traditionally gotten its phone calls returned nor had any affordable solution. Truly, *any* American with meaningful assets should be operating off of his or her own financial plan and should be checking back with that plan on a regular basis once a year. Yet how many have any plan at all? If you're interested in more on TMF Money Advisor, visit TMFMA.Fool.com.

Getting good people involved in your money means in most cases finding independent financial advice, the only kind that can have you and your own best interests at its heart. Up until now, Americans have been too content to get their questions answered by salesmen. We go to buy a new car. We ask our salesman, "Which one do you think I should get?" We ask commission-driven brokers to educate us about investing, failing to consider seriously enough that this person is obviously being paid for every trade made on every customer account. A lot of us have been too content to accept *dependent* advice, advice that is dependent on your transaction to generate fees for your friendly advisor.

Many have come to us with some version of this: "Guys, I've been on Fool.com, have actively followed your discussion boards for some time, and have learned more in the past few months than I did in my two years of getting an MBA. Here's my situation: I am twenty-nine years old and two years ago I got sold an annuity. So my money is now locked in at low rates of return paying pretty high fees for twenty years! And I'd have to pay a steep penalty to get out of it. The problem is, I didn't know what I was doing at the time I was sold on it by some salesman, and now I can see it's a real mistake for me."

And for a lot of people, particularly younger people, it would be. And yet that is just one sort of mistake frequently made. And why? Because again, we haven't surrounded ourselves with great people.

# 14

# Know How You Make Money

**Common** sense ain't that common.

If it were, brimming self-help bookshelves would be less brimming, and nearby you'd find far fewer finance and business books too. But fortunately for finance author hacks like us, it's as the wag says: Common sense ain't that common.

Take our point this chapter: *Know how you make money*. You'd think that participants in business and investing, prior to getting involved with either, would have strictly sought out how to make money and entered the game with their eyes wide open. You *would* think that, certainly. But the wreckage of failed Internet hopes and dreams makes it clear that most went in, like the 1999 Kubrick flick, with eyes wide shut.

Not to make light of this, but when Kubrick himself presented Warner Bros. with the final cut of his film *Eyes Wide Shut,* he died four days later.

We can't afford eyes wide shut, as we prepare for the future with stronger resolutions, built on foundations of learning from the past and doing in the present. Been there, done that. If you're going to talk business and investing, you really must know how you'll make money. Go in with a plan. You may not be correct from the start, but you can modify your approach based on what you learn as you go.

## THE BUSINESS LESSON

Contrary to the now popular view that they were motivated by greed and megalomaniacal ambition, many departed Internet businesses were actually conceived of by passionate, caring, and independent-thinking people who genuinely believed they were creating something beneficial and sustainable. And in many cases they were. They had a service aim.

But alas, they didn't really think about how their company would generate profit. Or if they did, their answers in retrospect look exceedingly fanciful, castles in the sky. They didn't accurately answer some tough questions: What will cause our customers to pay significantly above our own costs in order to net us a profit? And what is therefore the most effective way we should be using our time? As we wrote earlier in the book, we realized the importance of such questions regrettably late in our own corporate history. "Who is paying us? Who are our customers?" We finally began asking, long about year six. This profit questing is and should be an ongoing and never-ending process at all companies, great and small. The initial challenge for many entrepreneurs is to start that process in earnest!

We owe it to those we work with, manage, or report to in business to know how our company earns a profit. A good example of a bad company over the past several years is one we mentioned earlier in Chapter 4, Lucent Technologies, which over the course of 2000–2001 imploded, dropping from $80 to $7. Prior to the dramatic sell-off it had been one of the most widely held stocks in America, the former Bell Labs, a high-tech spin-off from AT&T.

Ask yourself this: How many people who owned Lucent really knew much about it? Could these employees or shareholders have explained the company's business model in two minutes or less? Did they have any sort of grip on the product lines that led to the revenue lines? Or did many investors just buy a high-tech name and leave it at that?

We think it's the latter. We're not at all convinced that most people knew how this company made money. We think it's clear in retrospect that even management itself didn't know how to make money. And if all these people didn't know how the company made money, they were unprepared to detect when the company *stopped* making it. The reason we don't believe that most people knew how Lucent made money is that if you were watching its financial statements, you saw *well ahead of time* the real misalignment that was occurring between the company's actions and the profit emerging from those actions. Had you been watching this, and clearly most Americans, including many institutional money managers, were not, you would have avoided huge losses as an investor, losses that wound up equating to an astounding $200 billion in disappearing market cap. We'll pat our Fool HQ editorial team on the back here, because they were warning readers with every passing earnings release.

Especially for big companies, we like to keep a really tight focus on the balance sheet. (If you are unfamiliar with how to read financial statements, pick up *The Motley Fool Investment Guide* next time you're at the bookstore, or point your Internet browser to FoolMart.com for our online seminar "Crack the Code: Read Financial Statements Like a Pro.") Whether you work for a company, invest in it, or both, know your company's balance sheet. In Lucent's case, its balance sheet contained at least two telling items. The first was the company's inventory, which was growing at a pace far exceeding overall sales growth—not a good sign, as it suggested that the company was cranking out too much product. The second was the company's accounts receivable, which were growing rapidly, as well. This indicated that Lucent was signing contracts but not actually getting paid money from those contracts anytime soon, or in some cases (as it turned out), at all. However, in a standard accounting practice, it *could* still announce these contracts as sales *and* book the consequent earnings. Thus, the company could continue for a while to broadcast that it was meeting its sales and earnings promises to Wall Street. "Look, they beat their earnings estimates!" one investor could celebrate over drinks with another. "They even beat the whisper number!" (The whisper number is the supposedly more accurate earnings estimate known only by *those in the know*. Pardon our skepticism, given that these numbers are regularly published in newsletters and on Web sites.)

In point of fact, however, Lucent was beginning to fail, beginning to expose how truly horribly the company was being managed, beginning to prepare its stock for an eventual drop of more than 90 percent, shaving off what may be a historical record of market capitalization in fairly short order.

This outcome was not dissimilar to what happened to MicroStrategy, the Internet software seller that was reporting big numbers by signing multiyear software contracts and announcing all the numbers up front, as if it had been paid ALL monies from the life of a five-year contract on day one. When the SEC started a-calling, the stock began a steep fall from $330 at its high to $4, as of this writing. That 98.8 percent loss represents a drop in market capitalization from $14 billion to just $172 million. That $172 million looks even smaller when you consider that CEO Michael Saylor grabbed headlines in March 2000 by pledging $100 million of his stock toward creation of an online university, obtaining several endorsements from U.S. senators and announcing the education would be for free. Fools might wonder whether they were going to be teaching . . . accounting?

Obviously, Enron is another company that comes quickly to mind as a spectacular flop largely mirroring these same story lines. We could go on about this, but we think you get the point: Where were the whistle-blowers? Were the people working at these companies ignorant of what was happening, or merely criminal? Perhaps America needs more people like Sherron Watkins, Enron's vice president of corporate development who wrote Chairman Ken Lay in August of 2001 complaining about the energy company's "veil of secrecy" blanketing its "funny accounting" and that she feared these financial practices might cause Enron to "implode in a wave of accounting scandals."

Lucent and MicroStrategy and Enron were acting in a way that would grab headlines, please Wall Street, briefly enrich management, and that would absolutely *not* create *sustainable profit*. They were either trying to fluff up their numbers or they didn't really know what they were doing, or in some cases perhaps both. Companies will often create incentives for their salespeople to go and get the sale done to meet the quarterly numbers and, in Lucent's case, who cares if you can't get the money up front? Or in MicroStrategy's case, hey, just announce it *as if* we got all the money up front. When customers later decide they don't want to follow through on some or all of the contract, or can't afford it anymore, that really hurts companies like Lucent and its investors, and proves once again why conservative accounting provides a worthy standard.

But again, if you don't know much about accounting—and how many of Lucent's investors were wise to this?—you are far less prepared to make intelligent decisions about how your money is invested. You need to know how your company makes money, and to know that, you have to be able to read financial statements.

Peter Drucker said 90 percent of the work that he has seen in American corporations over the last fifteen years has been spent creating 10 percent of the profit. He feels there is tremendous misalignment of resources at most companies, effort that fails to drive toward the ultimate aim of the business. Both GE's Welch and Coca-Cola's former CEO, the late Roberto Goizueta, have repeatedly emphasized what that ultimate aim is: to make profits. You incorporate for a reason, they have said. If making money for your investors is not your aim, set up your organization as learning-centered or not-for-profit. But once you start taking investor capital, the primary aim of the organization is to maximize value for the investors. If that isn't suitable for the people working in that particular organization, either encourage them to move or change your structure.

If you're going to incorporate and try to make money, you better become as quickly as possible a student of how the organization will make money, an enthusiast on the subject, an authority. And if things aren't going as planned, be like

Enron's Sherron Watkins. Acknowledge problems, work to fix them. But again, you have to understand how an entity is making money (or its plans to do so) before you can possibly be knowledgeable enough to criticize it or correct it.

## THE INVESTING LESSON

Know How You Make Money means a related but different thing to investors. By now it goes without saying that you have to understand the business model of any company you're invested in; we've been over that territory. But as an investor, you also need to know how *you* make money.

The way to make money in the stock market is over time. There's really no dependable way around it. Okay, you might get lucky. You might hit a five-year grand slam, and maybe re- tire off of that. And certainly we have had people come up and shake our hands and say they took early retirement be- cause of this stock or that idea. But that is an anomaly, and as an investment approach is far more likely to fail (in quite a costly way, if you've loaded your money into one investment) than to succeed.

So the real way to make money is by staying invested over time, and investing more every two weeks—some portion of your paycheck, ideally 5 percent to 10 percent—through good markets and bad. Invest in your retirement plan at work, tak- ing advantage of tax deferment. If you have extra savings left over, create your own private portfolio. In both cases, you're using the power of compounding. Remember that $1,000 in- vested for a child at birth, sixty-five years later, through just sheer compounding at historical market averages (in an index fund), becomes $1 million. Now $1 million sixty-five years from now won't quite have the purchasing power it has today, but it's not a bad sum considering no money was ever added and the beneficiary did no work whatsoever (and neither did you) to grow it. The *money* was doing the work, over the years—a very pleasing prospect. Even more pleasing is if you can afford to stow away more. Maybe rather than invest $1,000 you can afford to invest $10,000? Maybe rather than just the index fund you earn a higher return mixing in some market-beating stocks?

Know how you make money as an investor: You make that money over time.

One story, written by Motley Fool community member B50000, illustrates this lesson beautifully. This particular one, published at Fool.com on October 6, 1999, was entitled "The 50,000 Percent Milestone." Here is an excerpt:

> This past Monday, one of my stocks touched a milestone. The overall gain on this stock crossed the 50,000 percent mark. I'll bet you'd like to know how I found it. . . .
>
> My wife's grandfather and great-grandfather started a business about sixty years ago. Her grandfather worked it for sixty years. He was over ninety when he died, having worked there until the last year of his life. He lived frugally but comfortably in the same house for most of that time.
>
> Over the course of her life, my wife received some stock in the family business from her grandmother and grandfather. Her grandfather, in his final years, gave the maximum $10,000 tax-free annual gift to each of us and to our children in the form of stock in the family business. The business was sold to a publicly traded company the year before he died. The sale of the business dramatically increased the value of these gifts. And since the sale, the stock has more than doubled.
>
> The receipt and management of this amazing gift was what brought me to The Fool. Realizing that I knew nothing about how to deal with this windfall, I searched for help. I understood the inherent conflict of interest that financial salespeople work under. So I managed to avoid anyone who worked on commission and instead ended up at the doorstep of a fee-only financial planner. Her advice: Sell it all and invest in a combination of mutual funds selected by her screening program. At $75 per hour, I considered this advice to be severely overpriced. . . .

I read. I researched. I talked to people. But I just wasn't finding the solid advice I wanted. I had heard of The Fool, but it seemed too good to be true. It just seemed like another scam to get rich. But, having exhausted all other avenues, this student, now ready, gave in and read The Fool. . . .

We've learned about the slow and steady road to wealth, the tax advantages of letting your winners run, mechanical methods, and valuing potential investments. . . . We've also given some of the stock away. But much remains unsold and sits as stark evidence to the benefits of buy and hold, proof of the magic of compounding.

As I mentioned, the gain on the stock now stands at better than 50,000 percent. Our personal gain is immeasurable. My wife's grandfather has provided us with the ability to do virtually anything we desire. It's an opportunity we never imagined. As a result, we have been able to help family members, friends, and our favorite charities as well as upgrade our lives a little. We still try to live below our means (meaning my salary), though that's never been our strong suit.

By the way, do you know what a 50,000 percent gain over sixty years works out to in compounded annual terms? About 10.9 percent a year. Sounds pretty close to the market average, doesn't it? I'm hoping to do even better over the next sixty years for my grandchildren. And I'm hoping to teach them how to save $75/hour and manage it themselves.

Sure enough, that family investment—as valuable as it wound up being over time—wasn't General Electric. It wasn't Coca-Cola, or any other incredibly lucrative, long-term-market-beating investment. This was an average company that performed at the market average. Of course, it was certainly *more* than average, given its longevity. But it was generating average returns.

The point is, know how you make money as an investor. The answer is, use time as your ally.

# 15
# Have Fun

Our final resolution as we proceed through year 2002 and beyond is very simple: Have Fun. You'll notice it works on both a business and investing level, and in a lot of other contexts besides. In business, hey, you're spending upward of eight hours a *day* at it. You better be having fun. One of the best decisions we ever made was to stop what we both were doing in 1994 and turn The Motley Fool into an online business. Prior to that, one of us was in grad school working on two boring degrees and one of us was working at a job he couldn't stand. We both decided to quit and take our love of investing and start our own thing, and it's been mostly champagne ever since even despite a horrendous last eighteen months. Most important, we will accept nothing less than entertaining work lives, and we've always endeavored to make Fool HQ the most fun office our employees could imagine, and still call work.

As investors, having fun equals making money by investing in companies you know and love. Can't have much more fun than that, as an investor. If investing *isn't* fun for you, remember, for any monies that you won't need for at least five years, go with the incredibly boring and unfun and rhythmless, gawky—and successful—index fund.

We're talking here of course about having fun in the future. What better inspiration to close with than stories coming from real people, fellow Fools from across the world (with Motley Fool screen names attached), who recently sent us missives about how they've had fun with their money *even through the difficult climate out of which we're only now emerging.* So these inspired and inspiring people—nay, *investors,* picking up on a point made earlier, as we are *all* investors—have still managed to enjoy themselves through a horrible investing climate.

Pull up a chair, get a warm or cool drink (depending on the season), and relax with us, and let us have some fun together, and be reminded that no one is more directly responsible for fashioning a wonderful life for yourself than you. Yes, *fashioning!*

AUTHOR: GINNEY10306
How do I have fun with my money? I'm an eighty-year-old; my husband Bill is eighty-three. Do you think age stops us? Never.

We've taken our three granddaughters on vacation for the past ten years, every summer. Always a place of their choice. Our daughter does the driving, and *we pay!* That's the secret. We've traveled across the United States, Holland, France, and Spain. Our whole family has been learning how the rest of the world lives. My husband and I, we just plain enjoy! Here's the beauty of it. My husband and I never lift a suitcase. We get door-to-door service. We rent the finest car possible. My attitude is "If someone else can do it, so can I."

All of this money was made in the market, and I had fun earning it. What's more—I'm still doing it! I'm a bit of a gambler, but I play to win. I've invested in fuel cell companies and nanotechnology. It will take a while for brokers to catch on. I bought Human Genome and PerkinElmer in their infancy. Never listen to big-time brokers! They offer advice after they got in and made theirs.

AUTHOR: SPENCERSDADA
December 24, 2001, is my mother's sixtieth birthday. My five brothers are
all planning a big party for her in Boston on the 22nd. Since I live in Florida
I hadn't planned on going; we already had plans to drive to Virginia to my
in-laws. It was too much trouble. It would be too expensive.

But then I started to feel like I was missing out on one of the few
chances for us all to be together. I began looking for a way to go. I knew
we couldn't afford a trip for my wife and two kids (Spencer, age four,
Gracie, almost two), but I thought I could go alone. Then my wife
suggested that my four-year-old son go too if we found cheap enough
flights. Great idea! The last time he and I had a weekend alone was when
he was four months old.

My wife got online and started looking up airfares. Amazingly, she found
flights from Baltimore to Boston for only $82.50 round-trip! We have a
four-hour drive from Virginia to Baltimore, but for that price it's worth
it. As I looked further I found ways to make this trip fun but cheap.
How? Taking the T subway from the airport, $1 each. For my son it'll be
an adventure. Then we'll stay on my brother's couch, no charge. Another
adventure. And tickets for the Boston Museum of Science and the Boston
Children's Museum, free because we're members of the Florida Museum
of Natural History. And a winter coat for my son, $35 on sale at
Gymboree.com. And hats and mittens free from my brother (what can I
say, we live in Florida). All these, adventures for my son.

The most important thing to me is that I get a weekend with my family,
and particularly a chance to forge a new bond with my son. I'm doing it
cheap, but then again, it'll be priceless.

AUTHOR: THERESA105
My favorite activities for years and years have been reading, watching
movies, listening to music, and taking long walks. With the aid of the
public library, the first two activities cost me *nothing!* I think public
libraries are the best use of tax dollars that there is.

At the one here in Seattle, videos are free to check out for *three weeks*.
There's a long waiting list for new releases but not for the older ones. I

love the comedies of the 1930s and 1940s. I love movies set in foreign countries; peeks into other cultures and other ways of looking at things.

If I was renting the amount of videos I watch from Blockbuster, instead of getting them from the library for free, I'm sure it'd cost me at least a thousand dollars per year. And books—there are *so* many great books out there. It would take several lifetimes to read them all. All free at the library.

AUTHOR: AMSTARK

This year, in the midst of a business slowdown, I decided to use a month of my banked vacation time to visit a new continent. I visited Zambia in southern central Africa.

The airfare was a bit pricey, but living expenses were minimal. I stayed the month with a missionary family my church supports. It was a great cultural immersion. I spent the weekdays working on a church construction site, digging footers and pouring concrete with Zambians happy to work a hard nine hours for 7,000 kwacha a day (that's about $2).

One Sunday I tented with a couple of my Zambian friends in a farming village that was about an hour's bike ride down a narrow sandy path from town. We spent that evening sitting around a campfire, singing Bemba songs, and talking (with the help of my friends who spoke Bemba and English). Our hosts served us a feast of nshima (dried fish with a relish), boiled yams, and roasted peanuts for dessert. In the morning I woke up to the obnoxious crowing of roosters right outside my tent.

At the end of my trip I spent a couple of days at South Luangwa Safari Park, enjoying an astonishing abundance of animal life. It was an amazing vacation. Fun, stimulating, exciting, mind-opening, and challenging all at once. Oh, yes, and since I was Foolishly doing work for a charitable organization—it was all tax-deductible.

AUTHOR: SCDELANEY

If I could drop a coin in a machine and learn the date of my death, I'd do it in a heartbeat. That's the wild card of retirement investing. Since we don't know how long we'll be around, we really don't know how much money we'll need—if any at all. Thanks to incredible salary jumps, my wife and I live well below our means. We've been investing substantial amounts in our retirement accounts these past few years. Over the summer we've had many conversations about what we'd like to do. Naturally my wife's first idea was to buy a bigger house. My thought was that our modest house was fine. We have 1,570 square feet, five- and three-year-old daughters, and a dog. That's an amazing 314 square feet per family member! Although we agreed it might get crowded in those teen years, we thought we could survive.

My wife's next idea was to buy a sailboat. If I knew how she came up with this idea, I'd probably market it. Neither of us had owned a boat before, but we wanted one we could sail around and sleep on. We thought we could spend around $30,000 on a used one. Although I've sailed before, my wife hadn't. She signed up for a two-weekend sailing class so we could be sure sailing was something she wanted to do. We talked to some friends and looked around quite a bit. Eventually we learned that we liked the newer boats. Our ballpark cost escalated. We both got a bit gun-shy when we realized how much money we were talking about.

On September 7, 1985, my father had died suddenly of a heart attack and was buried on the 13th, my twenty-first birthday. My favorite memories of my father are the stupid ones like playing golf with him as a teenager on Friday afternoons or catching his fish on his pole when he asked me to hold it for a second while he went to get lunch. On September 11, 2001, my wife and I decided that we'd never leave each other mad, never leave the kids without telling them we love them, and that spending quality family time on a sailboat would leave our daughters with a lifetime of memories.

And so, on October 5, we went to the Annapolis, Maryland, sailboat show and ordered a new thirty-five-foot sailboat, paying more for the boat than we did for our house six years ago. Our decision to stay in our modest home will allow us to own the boat and continue to invest in our retirement as well as the kids' college fund.

Since I can't yet write about the fun my family and I will have sailing on the Chesapeake Bay next season, I'll stop for now.

AUTHOR: CLONES
My wife had been planning to buy me LASIK surgery to correct my vision for several months before Christmas. I'd done a lot of research on it myself, even at one point buying some VISX (now EYE) stock. I became comfortable with the procedure a couple of years ago, but was waiting for WavePrint mapping software and tracking lasers to come into regular use.

Then our country was attacked by terrorists. Our weak economy was shaken. The stock markets suffered. Our holdings declined.

I had my laser surgery last Friday. I see better now than any time since third grade when I first got glasses. Back then, I came home crying from school when I sat on my glasses and ruined them the first week of being a "four-eyes." Waking up in the morning and seeing the clock is amazing. Just walking around and seeing things unaided by corrective lenses is a miracle for me.

We're now planning a trip this summer to Pamplona, Spain, with another couple to participate in the Fiestas of San Fermín. I'm actually going to run with the bulls one morning with my friend. We'll be there for almost two weeks with time spent in Pamplona and Barcelona in Spain, along the Mediterranean in the South of France near Nice and Cannes, and finishing up on Bastille Day in Paris, where my wife was born and lived for the first five years of her life. It is the dream trip of a lifetime for us.

"Why are they spending so much money in such a turbulent economic time? Didn't he say earlier that his portfolio had lost value in the stock market?"

I am still a very valuable resource at my company and my salary isn't going to decrease. My wife is still teaching French in high school and it doesn't look like she'll get laid off anytime soon. We have been planning on our extravagances, our fun, our trips, our surgeries for quite a while

and our income has not changed and doesn't look like it will anytime
soon. We saved the money already and there is no reason to change our
spending plans when our income hasn't changed. Okay, so our stock
holdings are worth less now than last year or even two years ago. We
didn't need that money for at least three to five years anyway, which was
why we invested it.

Unless we see a good reason to change our lifestyle choices, we'll
continue to plan fun and good things for our life, we'll save our money
for those things, and we'll continue to invest money. We're just buying
stock at bargain basement prices now!

## AUTHOR: PWYLES

What do we do for fun in a bear market? That's easy—the same things
we do for fun in a bull market.

During the spring and summer, every other weekend, we hitch up the
tent trailer and go camping. We've taken the trailer out in the fall, but
not winter yet (the key word there is *yet*). Here's what it costs:

| | |
|---|---|
| Quarter of a tank of gas | $ 5.00 |
| Campground fees (two nights) | $40.00 |
| Groceries | $20.00 |
| Dancing for hours at the campground to a live band | priceless |

or perhaps:

| | |
|---|---|
| Camping in national forest | $ 10.00 |
| Annual fishing license | $ 30.00 |
| Digital camera on eBay | $100.00 |
| Getting a picture of your daughter catching her first fish | priceless |

It doesn't matter that for the last eighteen months the bear has been
roaring on Wall Street, because the money there isn't needed yet. At best
it will be ten years until I can retire, so today's 401(k) money buys more
units in an index fund. At these lowered prices, it's buying me more

retirement. And until it's possible to take month-long trips with a trailer for fun, it'll be weekend trips with a trailer for fun. It doesn't matter what the bulls and bears are doing, what I'm doing is RVing. Fuel cost affects the cost of the trips more than Wall Street does, but even with the lofty fuel prices this summer the other costs were much higher.

Wonder what the weather will be like this weekend; I have some canvas that hasn't seen daylight for a while!

AUTHOR: MMTHOMPS
We have the most fun with our money when we give it away, trying to follow our rule to give a sum that might actually make a difference. We receive a number of circular letters from people who raise their own support for various missionary endeavors. Last year a couple we knew who work in Africa wrote that they needed to raise money to buy a "bull bar" for their jeep—which is just what it sounds like! We decided to give the whole amount they needed. We received not only a thank-you, but photographs showing the jeep in various interesting situations in Africa. These people, whom we had known a bit before, have now become better friends. When they were in the area recently, we shared a delightful evening together.

We try to involve our daughters, ages ten and fifteen, in making decisions about our charitable giving. We talked to them about the bull bar. At year's end, we tell them what sum of money we have to give, describe various charities we support, and ask for their input, and even let them make some of the allocations. We also explain to them what we are "giving up"—a new car, a trip, or whatever, so they have some idea of the value of this money. My husband and I find this immensely rewarding, even fun, and look forward to it every year.

AUTHOR: POLOSPORTX99
Cash Money Motto? Let's Spend Some More!

As I walk into the electronics department, the video game section pulls me over with its secret tractor beam. A Nintendo GameCube stares me in the eye and whispers in my ear, "Buy me, Aaron! Just buy me! You will be able to play *Tony Hawk 3* and *Star Wars Rogue Leader* all night long!"

I try to resist the temptations that build up inside me, but the system has me under its spell. The "Force" is strong with the Cube and all resistance is defeated, as I hand the cashier my Visa and they hand me my receipt. Buying video games is just one of the ways I have fun with my money. I also enjoy spending my hard-earned cash on snowboarding and long-term investments.

Growing up with video games and watching the systems evolve has been a part of my life. There were countless hours spent in front of the TV as I tried to get the most play time out of the *Final Fantasy* game I had rented at the local video store. Now that I am in college, I have to come up with my own money instead of my parents' to support this video game habit. Stereotypically, the college student is always poor and has thousands of dollars built up in debt and student loans. Luckily, I thought ahead as a teenager in order to avoid falling into this category. When I turned eighteen, I went to an Army recruiter and signed up to be in the local National Guard unit. Also, taking note of all the high-tech industries here, in Silicon Forest, I chose a military occupation in electronics. The year-long training proved to be well worth the wait, considering I currently have no college debts and I am working for LSI Logic. This evasion of college debt and this high-tech job provide me with plenty of money to enjoy my top-of-the-line video game experience!

I also love to blow my money, err, I mean spend my money on snowboarding. Snowboarding provides an entire day away from work and school, replacing it with immense fun! The only problem is that lift tickets cost between $40 to $50 per day. I have taken extreme cost-saving measures in order to help afford these outrageous lift ticket prices. An example of these cost-saving measures is as follows: I originally lived with my parents while I attended the local community college. During the summer, my parents decided that they would like to charge me rent of $500 for every two months. (But Mom and Dad, I am in college, where's your support?) This idea of my parents charging me rent opened up some new living options: I could either live with them and pay the $500 for every two months, or I could move in with a friend and pay $600 for every two months. I decided to take my friend up on his offer since it was only $50 a month more and I wouldn't have to be living with my parents. Since snowboarding season was months away, I had time to plan my funding. While I lived with my friend, I would frequently visit my parents' house and tell them about how good of a future investment I would be for them. I bragged about my consistently good grades and told them about how well I was doing at work. In the end, I was able to convince my parents to take me back in for free, saving me those hundreds of dollars in rent money so I can put it to use up on the mountain!

After having fun with my money on video games and snowboarding, I often feel that I am about to go broke. I decided that I ought to do something smart with the little bit of money left over and invest it. So, being the cheap person I am when it comes to paying fees to other people, I began to look into investing on my own and on developing new skills of how to manage my money. After reading books such as *A Random Walk Down Wall Street* and *Buffettology*, I realized that making my own intelligent investments wasn't as hard as I had originally imagined. Also inspired by Fool.com, I began to take an extreme liking to this new hobby of mine.

So next time I see that video game look me in the eye and tell me to buy it, am I going to be able to just walk away? Probably not. Until I lose my interest in snowboarding, which is as likely as my winning the lottery, I will also continue to have fun purchasing expensive lift tickets in order to surf down the slopes. With the majority of my money currently being put into snowboarding and video games, I am thankful to have discovered the fun in long-term investing and how it can help me manage my money better for the future. With the help of video games, snowboarding, and long-term investing, I have immense fun spending my money!

AUTHOR: AMAUGHAN
One of the best investments I made this year was a hot tub. It seemed frivolous at first, especially when contemplating where to locate a ton of water, pumps, and plastic. But it turned out well.

The addition of fifty ampere electrical service to the backyard and the eight-inch concrete pad to support it seemed, at the time, the ultimate waste of money and effort. On the other hand, the six-foot vinyl privacy fence I added to the backyard was probably needed anyway; the hot tub made it expedient.

I purchased the tub at a warehouse store, so I had to learn the hard way about what a hot tub is supposed to do, with jets and bubbles and ozone and chemicals and algae (I expect I probably have a few more lessons to learn).

In spite of all the cost, learning curve, and chemical smells, there's nothing like sitting in the backyard during a snowstorm, getting ice in your hair and watching the grandkids climb out to run around in the snow before jumping back in.

It's nice to know that somewhere, somehow, a hot tub company and a fencing company were able to keep someone working because I had saved to make this investment in life.

AUTHOR: JBFINS

Buffett, and I mean Jimmy not Warren, refers to dollar bills as "fun tickets." I think that's a wonderful characterization of something that all too often causes a tremendous stress in people's lives, mine in particular. You see my wife and I are newlyweds who are saving for a down payment on a house. Conservation of money is *priority one* for now. In our efforts to save for the biggest purchase of our lives, we've made several monetary sacrifices. That isn't to say that our efforts would make Henry David Thoreau proud, but we *have* fine-tuned our budget so that whatever is not necessary ain't acquired.

It's been a stressful endeavor, frugality. We are both working hard and find it difficult at times to relieve the stress that we voluntarily bring into our lives. In an effort to relieve the stress, I have decided to spend some "fun tickets" every day on flowers for my wife.

In Grand Central there is a woman who sells flowers on the train platforms. Her price ranges from $2 to $5, depending on how well you can negotiate. Every day, before I get on the train, I buy some flowers. I always smile when I pay her because she doesn't do a tremendous amount of business, and I feel proud to be one of her few customers. I am happy to know that I've given her some fun tickets to play with and in return she's given me something that'll bring a smile to my wife's face. Which is the real reward for me, because my wife's smile reminds me how wonderful life is, and that it really is just a game with no scorekeeper.

I know that it isn't the most "Foolish" thing to do, but I don't care. [Gardner Note: We disagree! This is very Foolish. Foolishness is lighthearted, sensible, imaginative, colorful . . . and certainly recognizes love as a greater force than money.] After a long day of work, I look forward to bartering with the flower lady and giving her my money hoping that it makes as much a difference in her life as it does in mine. If we have to wait a little longer to buy our house, then so be it. At least we'll wait with smiles on our faces.

AUTHOR: NAPAVALLEYFOOL
I'm a food and wine writer and my husband manages the tasting room of a Napa Valley winery. We're, obviously, deeply entrenched in the wine industry. After September 11, our household income was pole-axed as people reassessed their lives and pulled back from spending.

Then I got the news that my mother has been massively improvident and spent much of the investment capital she'd been living on. Found out her secret: that she's never—in all her life—bothered to look at the difference between income and outflow. I reallocated her investments and am now giving them five years to gain back some value from compound interest while I support her.

How could I possibly be having fun with my money, you ask?

My husband and I have been feeding our imaginations.

We wander bookstores picking up gems that we bring home and read to one another in the evenings by the fire. I'm doing big oil paintings of seductive pears and sensual flowers that fill my evenings with joy. I hand-carved a linoleum block to create our home-printed holiday cards, and am spending more time being creative than at any other time in my life.

We've also been getting to know more people in our community.

Those plans for replacing my rickety old '88 Subaru have been swapped for repairs to keep it chugging along, and the fellows down at the tiny garage that will be doing the work are wonderfully warm, funny guys that I'd never have gotten to know otherwise. Dinners at home with friends have replaced restaurant dining, and we measure the difference in relaxation and intimacy, not dollars.

It's been a good year—filled with change and challenge—but very good.

And so this book, like all others, comes to an end. But this last chapter was so pleasurable to compile and to read, and reread, that we will make a point of returning to it again and again. The range of humanity that verily breathes from the pages here . . . and so nobly! Finding pleasure in the face of strife . . . As we have written in one or two other places, money is opportunity. It is to be enjoyed—not all of it!—in the present. Some is to be set aside, piled high if possible, for a future need. And at one or more sometimes uncertain future points, it is to be brought out in times of need or trouble, for your rescue or someone else's—or, luckier yet, perhaps merely disbursed magnificently, spinning through a French countryside with your grandchildren on your knees, hanging a 720 with an electric blue snowboard over a sea of frosty, transfixed faces. Or handed as fun tickets to a woman who, every evening without fail, brings beauty to Grand Central Station and sends it out into smiles across Manhattan.

*What a piece of work is a man, how noble in reason, how infinite in faculties, in form and moving, how express and admirable in action, how like an angel in apprehension, how like a god: the beauty of the world, the paragon of animals. . . .*

# INDEX

# ADDITIONAL RESOURCES AT FOOL.COM

We hope you have enjoyed reading this book and that it has provided you with valuable and helpful information. Throughout the book, you have been pointed toward additional resources and services to help you in your quest to take control of your financial destiny. Fool.com offers many of these additional resources at your fingertips. Consider these services your Solution Centers, as they are oriented toward first educating you and then enabling you to take action. Below is an abbreviated but helpful list of some of the key areas, most of which have appeared in this book:

## Insurance Center—insurance.Fool.com

- Figure out what types of insurance you need, how much of it you should purchase, and how to get coverage at the lowest cost.

## Short-Term Savings Center—savings.Fool.com

- Determine how much cash to stash for emergencies and where to keep it.

## IRA Center—ira.Fool.com

- Plan your retirement, find out if you are eligible to invest in an IRA account, evaluate the options—traditional or Roth IRA—and learn how to open one.

## Index Center—indexcenter.Fool.com

- Learn about stock market indices, why they are important to use in comparison to your portfolio's performance, and how you can earn their investment returns.

## Fool School—Fool.com/school

- The Fool School area will get you started with the basics. Learn the 13 Steps to Investing Foolishly, the skinny on mutual funds, some beginner investing strategies such as dividend reinvestment plans and index funds.

## Fool Perks—register.Fool.com

- Fool Perks offers free specials from the Fool and its selected partners. Offers include sample trial subscriptions to financial and business publications, special bank CD rates, and discount broker premiums for opening an account.

## The Fool Community

The Fool Community is the place at Fool.com where members join together to interact, learn, question, and exchange ideas. The Community offers:

- Thousands of active conversations
- Staff-monitored discussions—comfortable and clean
- An opportunity to post messages to get your questions answered

To check out what other Fools are saying, take a peek with a 30-day free trial. To check it out, go online to boards.Fool.com.

## TMF Money Advisor

TMF Money Advisor provides personalized, objective advice for all aspects of your financial life. With TMF Money Advisor you get:

- Access to an unbiased, unconflicted financial advisor
- An online tool you can use to create a personal financial plan
- A collection of 10 world-class Motley Fool seminars

To learn more about the TMF Money Advisor service and its special offers go to: TMFMA.Fool.com.

The Motley Fool's aim is to help you find solutions to the many and sometimes complex matters of money and investing. Whether you're looking for financial planning assistance, research on the stocks in your portfolio, new investment ideas, information about 401(k)s and IRAs, money-saving tips when buying a car or home, minute-by-minute stock quotes, or a place just to talk to other investors, Fool.com has all of that and more—available twenty-four hours a day.

# ABOUT THE AUTHORS

David and Tom Gardner co-founded The Motley Fool, an Alexandria, Virginia–based multimedia company, in 1993. They started out publishing a modest investment newsletter for friends and family, started talking stocks online in the early days of AOL, then launched their own investment education Web site, Fool.com, in 1997.

Tom graduated with an honors degree in English and creative writing from Brown University, and has been formally trained in just about everything but finance. David graduated as a Morehead Scholar from the University of North Carolina at Chapel Hill. With many ideas and no regrets, he quit his job writing for *Louis Rukeyser's Wall Street* (the newsletter, not the TV show) in order to found The Motley Fool newsletter with his brother.

Today, The Motley Fool has grown into an international multimedia company offering financial solutions to millions of individuals worldwide seeking to make better financial decisions and improve their overall quality of life. Tom and David have coauthored four *New York Times* business bestsellers, including *The Motley Fool Investment Guide, The Motley Fool You Have More Than You Think,* and *The Motley Fool's Rule Breakers,*

*Rule Makers.* In addition to writing bestselling books, the Gardners oversee a nationally syndicated newspaper column, which is carried by more than 200 papers, and host a weekly radio program on NPR. The Gardners, once voted "Interactive Age's Entrepreneurs of the Year 1996," recently hosted the award-winning PBS show "The Motley Fool Money-Making, Life-Changing Special."